TIME FOR GOD

TIME
FOR
GOD

A GUIDE TO PRAYER

By
Jacques Philippe

auline
BOOKS & MEDIA

Boston

Library of Congress Cataloging-in-Publication Data

Philippe, Jacques, Rev.
  [Temps pour Dieu. English]
  Time for God : a guide to prayer / by Jacques Philippe.
      p. cm.
  Includes bibliographical references and index.
  ISBN 0-8198-7413-2 (pbk. : alk. paper)
  1. Prayer—Catholic Church. I. Title.

  BV210.3.P4613 2005
  248.3'2—dc22

                              2004031115

Cover design by Rosana Usselmann

Original edition published in French under the title *Du Temps Pour Dieu*; First English edition outside of the Philippines, 2005.

Based on a translation by Sinag Tala, 6/F GMA Lou-Bel Plaza, C. Roces Avenue cor. Bagtikan St., San Antonio Village 1203, Makati City, Philippines.

Published by Pauline Books & Media, 50 Saint Paul's Avenue, Boston, MA 02130-3491. Printed in U.S.A.

www.pauline.org

Pauline Books & Media is the publishing house of the Daughters of St. Paul, an international congregation of women religious serving the Church with the communications media.

1 2 3 4 5 6 7 8 9   11 10 09 08 07 06 05

CONTENTS

Introduction

In Western Catholic tradition, "prayer" is a form of supplication that consists in placing oneself in God's presence for a time with the desire to enter into a loving, intimate communion with him in the midst of silence and solitude. All the masters of the spiritual life believe that "to pray"—that is, to regularly engage in this form of supplication—is a privileged and indispensable means of attaining an authentic Christian life, to know and to love God, and to respond to the call to holiness addressed to each person.

Today many people are thirsting for God and desire to lead a profound and intense prayer life. They want to pray, but various obstacles arise that prevent them from seriously committing themselves to prayer and, even more, from persevering along this path. They often lack the courage and determination needed to begin, or feel lost because they do not know exactly how to go about praying. Perhaps, after repeated attempts, they become discouraged by difficulties and so abandon the practice of prayer. This is regrettable because perseverance in prayer, as all the saints experienced, is the narrow gate that opens us to the Kingdom of Heaven. Through it alone do we receive all the blessings that "no eye has seen, nor ear heard, nor the human heart conceived..." (1 Cor 2:9). Prayer is the source of true joy because those who pray always "taste and see that the Lord is good" (Ps 34:8). The person who prays finds the living water that Jesus promised: "Those who drink of the water that I will give them will never be thirsty" (Jn 4:14).

Convinced of this truth, I wish to offer some guidance and advice in this book—the simpler and more specific the better. My aim is to help those persons of good will who desire to pray, so that they may not feel daunted by the difficulties that inevitably arise.

Many works have been written on prayer. All the great contemplative souls have dealt with the subject matter more eloquently, and I will of course cite them often. Nonetheless, I believe that the Church's traditional teaching on this subject should be presented to the faithful in a simple way. It ought to be accessible to everyone and adapted to current language and sensibility, since God, in his wisdom, leads us to holiness through a different pedagogy than those of the past. It is this idea that moved me to write this book.

CHAPTER ONE

PRAYER IS A GRACE, NOT A TECHNIQUE

PRAYER IS NOT CHRISTIAN YOGA

In order to persevere in the prayer life, we must avoid straying onto false paths. It is, therefore, indispensable for us to understand the specific features of Christian prayer, which distinguish it from other spiritual activities, especially since today's materialism has provoked a cultural backlash characterized by a thirst for the mystical, of communicating with the Invisible. While this is good, it often springs from experiences that are deceiving and even harmful.

The first fundamental truth we must understand, and without which we cannot make progress, is that the life of prayer, or so-called contemplative prayer, is not the result of a technique; it is a gift we receive.

St. Jane Frances de Chantal said: "The best method of prayer is not to have any method, because prayer is not obtained by artificial means [or, as we might say today, through a technique] but through grace." In this sense, no "method" or fixed formula suffices for us to pray well. True contemplative prayer is a gift that God gives to us gratuitously, but we must learn how to receive it.

It is necessary to insist on this point, especially when Eastern methods of meditation, such as yoga or Zen, have become so popular, due to the modern mentality that reduces everything to a technique. Ultimately, this arises from the human temptation to manipulate life, including the spiritual life, at will. We may have a more or less conscious concept of prayer as a kind of Christian yoga whereby we attain progress through a process of concentration and recollection, the right breathing exercises and posture, and the repeated chanting of certain formulas. Once we have mastered these elements, we enter a "higher state of consciousness."

Nevertheless, this view, which underlies Eastern techniques, sometimes breeds an utterly mistaken idea of Christian prayer and the mystical life. It is an erroneous view because it depends on methods, which, in the final analysis, depend on human effort alone. ~~Instead, in Christianity everything depends on God's gift of grace~~. Any apparent similarities or connections between an Eastern ascetic and a Christian contemplative are at best superficial. When it comes down to the essentials, we are dealing with two completely different, even incompatible, worlds.[1]

There are basic differences: on the one hand a reliance on efforts that essentially depend on our abili-

---

1. For a deeper consideration of this point, see Fayard's *Des bords du Gange aux rives du Jourdain (From the Banks of the Ganges to the River Jordan)*. Note the essential difference between Christian spirituality and that inspired by a non-Christian Eastern erudition. The goal of the latter's spiritual itinerary is usually to attain the absolute "I," or union with the great "All," the elimination of suffering through the suppression of all desire and the dissolution of the individual. On the other hand, the ultimate end of Christian prayer life is different: to transform the self into God, who stands before the supplicant. It is a loving union of a person with the Person. A profound union that distinguishes the persons involved, so that mutual self-giving in love may take place.

It is therefore important to be wary of popular currents of thought that fall under the catch-all term, New Age, a modern form of syncretism that mixes astrology, reincarnation, and Eastern spirituality—a present-day version of Gnosticism that totally rejects the mystery of the Incarnation. At the bottom of it is the promise of illusory self-fulfillment that denies the need for grace, which runs exactly counter to what is explained in this book. New Age also fosters egoism because it never considers the intrinsic value of the "other," but only insofar as that "other" is an instrument to one's self-fulfillment. It is a world bereft of any real relationship with "another"—in a word, a world bereft of love.

ties, which may be discovered and developed through the proper meditation techniques, and on the other hand a reliance on God, who gives himself to us freely and gratuitously. In prayer a certain degree of human initiative and action have a role to play, but the entire edifice of prayer rests on God's initiative and grace. We cannot lose sight of the fact that there remains a constant and sometimes subtle temptation to base our spiritual life on our own efforts rather than on God's inexhaustible mercy. The consequences of this are many and very significant.

SOME IMMEDIATE CONSEQUENCES

The first point to consider is that we can neither exaggerate the importance of nor rely entirely on methods or spiritual exercises even if they help us to pray. This would be to center our prayer life on ourselves and not on God—precisely what we must avoid. Neither can we think that we will be free of difficulties or distractions once we have gone through a "training period" or mastered some "tricks of the trade." What will help us to advance and to grow in our spiritual life lies elsewhere, and this is fortunate because if the edifice of prayer were founded solely on our efforts, then we would not go very far. St. Teresa of Avila affirms that "the entire edifice of prayer is founded on humility," that is, on the conviction that we can do nothing by ourselves. Rather, it is God, and God alone, who is the source of all the good in our lives. This conviction can strike a blow to our pride, but it is also liberating, because the God who loves us will urge us on infinitely farther and higher than we could go through our own efforts.

This fundamental principle has another liberating consequence. Some people possess gifts and talents that others do not. Thus, if the life of prayer were a matter of technique, perhaps only a handful of "gifted" individuals would be able to reach the heights of contemplative prayer. Some people can more easily recollect themselves and dwell on beautiful thoughts, but this is not important. The person who is able to channel his or her entire character, talents, and weaknesses to faithfully respond to the prompting of divine grace is the person who is capable of living a deep prayer life. The call to prayer, to the mystical life, to union with God is as universal as the call to holiness, because we cannot achieve one without the other. No one is excluded. Jesus does not address an elite group when he says: "Pray always" (Lk 18:1), or, "Whenever you pray, go into your room and shut the door and pray to your Father in secret; and your Father who sees in secret will reward you" (Mt 6:6).

If prayer is not a matter of mastering a technique but of grace then what matters most is not methods or formulas, but the conditions that allow us to receive this gift. In fact, these conditions consist of certain interior attitudes or dispositions of the heart. What assure us of progress in prayer and make it fruitful are the interior dispositions with which we approach prayer leading us to pray. The primary task is to make an effort to acquire, maintain, and intensify these dispositions of the heart. All the rest is God's work. Let us now look at the more important interior attitudes.

FAITH AND TRUST:
THE FOUNDATION OF PRAYER

Faith is the first and most fundamental attitude for prayer. We cannot reiterate enough that prayer entails struggle, and faith is a necessary weapon.

Faith is the capacity of the believer to act not on impulses, prejudices, or ideas drawn from the environment, but on the word of God, who cannot lie. Thus understood, the virtue of faith is the basis of prayer. There are different ways of putting faith into action.

Faith in God's presence

When preparing to pray alone before God in a room, a chapel, or before the Blessed Sacrament, we must believe with all our heart that God is present there. God is beside us, regardless of our feelings, merits, preparation, ability to dwell on beautiful thoughts, or state of mind. God looks at us and loves us. God is there, not because we deserve it or feel it, but because he promised it: "Go into your room and shut the door and pray to your Father in secret" (Mt 6:6).

We may feel dry, miserable, or that God is not there and has abandoned us. However, we can never doubt his loving and welcoming presence before the person who prays: "Anyone who comes to me I will not drive away" (Jn 6:37). God is there even before we invoke his presence, because he is the one who has invited us to that encounter. God, who is our Father, awaits us and tries to enter into communion with us. God desires us infinitely more than we desire him.

Faith that we are called to be united with God in prayer
Despite our difficulties, resistance, or objections, we should firmly believe that without exception everyone—the wise as well as the ignorant, the just as well as the sinner, the emotionally whole as well as the broken—is called to a prayer life where God speaks with us. God, who is just, calls us and will give us the graces needed to persevere and make our prayer life a profound and marvelous experience of intimate communion. Prayer is not reserved for the "spiritual elite."

The idea that "it's not for me" or "it's only for holy people, people who are better than me," contradicts the Gospel. We must believe that despite our difficulties and weaknesses, God will give us the needed strength to persevere.

Faith gives fruitfulness to prayer

The Lord calls us to a prayer life because it is a source of infinite blessings for us. It transforms us interiorly, sanctifies us, heals us, allows us to know and to love God, and makes us fervent and generous in loving others. The beginner must be convinced that in persevering she or he will receive all this and much more. Sometimes it may seem just the opposite: our prayer is sterile or tedious and things do not change. We must not lose heart even if it seems that the fruits of prayer elude us. Rather, we must keep at it with the certainty that God will keep his promise: "So I say to you, ask, and it will be given you; search, and you will find; knock, and the door will be opened for you. For everyone who asks receives, and everyone who searches finds, and for everyone who knocks, the door will be opened" (Lk 11:9–10). Those who persevere with confidence receive infinitely more than they could have dared to ask or hope for not because they deserve it, but because God has promised.

Still, it is a common temptation to stop praying when we do not receive the fruits as quickly as we expected. We must immediately reject this temptation with the faith that in time the divine promise will be fulfilled. "Be patient, therefore, beloved, until the coming of the Lord. The farmer waits for the precious crop from the earth, being patient with it until it receives the early and the late rains. You also must be patient: Strengthen your hearts, for the coming of the Lord is near" (Jas 5:7–8).

FIDELITY AND PERSEVERANCE

Whoever walks the path of prayer must first struggle to be faithful. It is not as important to experience moments of prayer that are beautiful and satisfying, rich in profound thoughts or sentiments, as it is to be faithful and persevering in prayer. In other words, we must not focus so much on the "quality" but on our fidelity to prayer. Quality will be the fruit of fidelity. Times of arid, impoverished, distracted, or relatively brief prayer, if practiced faithfully every day, are more meritorious and bear more fruit than long, ardent prayers offered inconsistently when we feel the circumstances conducive. After seriously committing ourselves to the life of prayer, the first battle we must win is fidelity at all costs, according to the rhythm we have established for ourselves. This is not an easy

victory. The devil knows the dangers for us and so
tries to dissuade us the best he can. He knows that a
person who is faithful to prayer can easily slip through
his fingers or, at least, will slip through one day. For
this reason, the devil will do everything and anything
to hinder us from fidelity to prayer. This will be treat-
ed further, but for the moment, bear in mind that an
hour of prayer poorly spent, but done with regularity
and fidelity, is more valuable than rare sublime
moments. Fidelity, and nothing else, gains for us all the
marvelous fruits of prayer.

Here must be repeated the fact that prayer is only
an exercise in loving God. And for human beings,
immersed in time, there is no real love without fidelity. How can we try to love God if we are not faithful
to encountering God every day in prayer?

PURITY OF INTENTION

After faith and fidelity, which we express concretely in
prayer, another fundamental attitude needed to persevere in prayer is *purity of intention.* Jesus said, "Blessed
are the pure in heart, for they will see God" (Mt 5:8).
According to the Gospel, the pure of heart are not
those who have never sinned and are beyond reproach,
but those who sincerely desire to forget themselves in
order to please God in everything. Thus, prayer is not

a self-centered search for pleasure, but the desire to please God. If this is not our aim, we will not persevere in prayer. If we seek our own satisfaction, we will abandon prayer as soon as it becomes too difficult, or when we feel dryness and discontent, or when we no longer draw from prayer the pleasure we had expected. Love is true and pure when the lover does not seek his or her own interests but those of the beloved, making the loved one happy. Therefore, we do not pray because of the pleasure or benefits drawn from it—even if these are immense—but primarily because we want to please God, who asks us to pray. We pray not for our own delight, but for God's.

This purity of intention is demanding but also sweet and liberating. They who seek themselves will easily lose heart and become restless when prayer no longer "works." A person who loves God with absolute purity remains calm when prayer becomes difficult or unsatisfying. Rather, he or she is immediately consoled with the thought that what matters is generously giving that moment to God in order to please him.

This is a very beautiful thing, but who is capable of loving God with such purity? Purity of intention, as already described, is indispensable, but we must understand that it cannot be fully acquired on the first steps along the spiritual life. We are only asked to consciously aim for this purity of intention and to practice it the best way we can in times of aridity. The truth is everyone who sets off on the spiritual journey seeks God, but also in part herself or himself. This is not a serious obstacle, but we must always aspire to a purer love.

This point helps us to unmask a trick of the devil, who can play prosecutor in our case to disturb us and dash our hopes to pieces. He presents disheartening evidence that our love for God is still very weak and imperfect, and that our spiritual life is only a self-seeking endeavor.

However, these thoughts should not shake us even if it does seem we are only seeking ourselves in prayer. Rather, with all simplicity we should show God that we desire to love him with a pure and disinterested love and then abandon ourselves to him with confidence, because he will take care of purifying us. To attempt to do this alone would be mere presumption, for if we attempt to uproot the weeds before the due time, we risk destroying the wheat as well (cf. Mt 12:20–34). Let us allow God's grace to work; let us be satisfied with persevering and patiently bearing with the dryness of soul that God allows so that our love for him may be purified.

The devil can also try to discourage us by suggesting to us that our prayer cannot please God because we are so full of miseries and defects. To this we must answer with a truth that is the heart of the Gospel and, as the Holy Spirit reminds us of through St. Thérèse of Lisieux, we do not please God with our merits and virtues, but, above all, with our boundless confidence in his mercy.

HUMILITY AND SPIRITUAL POVERTY

St. Teresa of Avila said, "The entire edifice of prayer is based on humility." This echoes what has been affirmed thus far: prayer is not founded on human ability but on the action of divine grace. In addition, Sacred Scripture states that: "God opposes the proud, but gives grace to the humble" (1 Pt 5:5). Humility is part of that basic attitude of heart without which it is impossible to persevere in prayer.

Humility is the capacity to calmly accept our essential poverty and to trust God in everything. The humble person cheerfully accepts that he or she is nothing because God is everything. He or she does not think that his or her misery is such a disaster; rather, it is an opportunity for God to work his great mercy in him or her.

Without humility, we cannot persevere in prayer. Prayer is inevitably an experience of poverty, detachment, and vulnerability. Other spiritual or pious practices may provide us with a crutch because it makes use of a particular aptitude or we have the feeling that we are doing something useful. It is also possible to rely on others when it comes to praying as a group or community. However, in the solitude and silence of personal prayer, we find ourselves face to face with God with nothing but our misery. It is difficult to accept our misery, and for this reason we naturally tend to flee silence. In prayer, however, it is impossible to avoid feeling inadequate. Although we may often taste God's sweetness and tenderness in prayer, usually it is our wretchedness, inability to pray, concerns, distractions, the memory of old hurts, faults, and failings, or our insecurities over the future that are all laid before our eyes. Thus, we find a thousand reasons to escape the stillness that unveils our radical nothingness before God. Indeed, we may refuse to accept our poverty and fragility. However, a trusting and cheerful acknowledgement of these is the source of all spiritual blessings: "Blessed are the poor in spirit, for theirs is the kingdom of heaven" (Mt 5:3).

Humble persons persevere in the life of prayer without presumption or self-reliance. They do not think themselves deserving of anything and are convinced that they cannot do anything by their own effort. The experience of constant frailty, difficulties, and falls are not surprising to humble persons; they bear these calmly, without becoming agitated, because they place all their hope in God, certain that divine mercy will obtain for them all that they are powerless to obtain or merit through their own efforts.

Now, since humble persons do not trust themselves, they are never disheartened—and this is what ultimately matters. And, as Fr. Francis Libermann once said, it is through discouragement that souls are lost. Thus, true humility and confidence go hand-in-hand.

We must never allow ourselves to feel shaken by our lukewarm or small love for God. At times, the beginner in the spiritual life can become discouraged when reading the life and works of the saints. When we read their ardent expressions of love for God, we may feel ourselves to be far from the goal and that we can never reach their level of spiritual fervor. This is a very common temptation. Let us persevere in our good desires and trust in God. God will put that love in our hearts. A strong and fervent love for God is not a natural thing, but the Holy Spirit enkindles it in the hearts of those who are persistent in asking, like the widow in the Gospel. Those who experience great feelings of love at the beginning do not always soar to great heights in the spiritual life.

THE DETERMINATION TO PERSEVERE

We may deduce that the main struggle in prayer is that of perseverance. God will grant us the grace of perseverance if we ask him for it with trust and firmly decide to apply ourselves.

We need a great deal of determination, especially at the beginning. St. Teresa of Avila insists on this:

> Let us now turn to those who wish to travel this road without rest until the end, which is the place where they can drink of the water of life. I repeat that the beginning is most important; everything depends on the firm resolve not to stop until they reach their goal, whatever may come, whatever may happen to them, however hard they may have to labor, whatever people may say of them, on the condition that they arrive even if they should die on the road, or lose heart before the trials they meet, whether the world dissolves before them.[2]

There is no sanctity without prayer

At this point, we shall treat of some considerations aimed at strengthening this determination and uncovering the traps, false reasons, or temptations that may shake it.

---

2. St. Teresa of Avila, *The Way of Perfection,* trans. and ed. by E. Allison Peers, from the critical edition of F. Silverio de Santa Teresa, O.C.D. (New York: Image Books, 1964), chap. 21.

In the first place, we must be convinced of the vital importance of prayer. St. John of the Cross said, "The one who flees from prayer, flees from everything that is good." All the saints prayed, and those who gave themselves most fully to the service of their neighbor were those who were most given to contemplation. St. Vincent de Paul, for instance, began each day with two to three hours of prayer.

It is impossible to make progress in the spiritual life without prayer. We can experience the most powerful moments of conversion and fervor after receiving a tremendous amount of grace, but, without fidelity to prayer, our Christian life would soon reach a dead end. For without prayer, we cannot receive the help we need from God to become holy, to undergo a deep interior transformation. The testimony of the saints is unanimous in this regard.

One may object that God bestows sanctifying grace on us and does so, principally, through the sacraments. Moreover, the Mass in itself is more important than personal prayer. This may be true, but without a prayer life, the sacraments would have a limited effect. The sacraments confer grace, but their effects are stunted because they do not find "good soil" in which to take root. We can ask ourselves, for example, why those who frequently receive Holy Communion are not holier. Often the reason is the absence of prayer in their life. The Holy Eucharist does not effect within the soul the healing and fruits it should because it is not welcomed with ardent faith, love, and adoration. The same is true with the other sacraments.

Those who do not pray habitually, no matter how faith-filled or pious, will not achieve full spiritual maturity. They will not acquire peace of soul because they will always experience excessive disquietude and view things according to their human or worldly significance. Thus, they will always suffer from vanity, selfishness, self-centeredness, ambition, meanness of heart, judgment, and an unhealthy willfulness and attachment to their opinions. Those who do not pray may acquire human wisdom and prudence, but not true spiritual freedom or a deep and radical purification of heart. They will not be able to grasp the depths of divine mercy or know how to make it known to others. Their judgments will always end up shortsighted, mistaken, and contemptible. They will never be able to walk God's ways, which are far different from what many—even those who have committed themselves to a life in the spirit—imagine them to be.

For example, some people who have participated in the charismatic renewal movement became perfect models of conversion. The Holy Spirit infuses them with a shining and touching encounter with God. However, after months or years of walking this fervent path, they reach a spiritual plateau and their vitality fades. What happens? Has God withdrawn his hand? Of course not, for "the gifts and the calling of God are irrevocable" (Rom 11:29). These persons simply did not know how to keep their hearts open to God's grace through a prayer life.

The problem of time

"I would like to pray, but I don't have the time." This is an often-heard excuse! It is true that in our world, overwhelmed with activity, there is real difficulty finding time for everything. Nevertheless, time is not the real problem. Rather, the problem lies in recognizing what matters most in life. As one contemporary author, Fr. Descouvemont, observed with amusement, no one ever died of hunger because of not having time to eat. There is always time to engage in vital activities, or, to put it another way, one "makes time." Thus, before we say that we do not have time to pray, we must review our priorities. What do I value most in life?

One of the greatest tragedies of our times is our inability to spend time with others, of "being there" for others—a reality that has caused great emotional wounds. Many children have closed in on themselves because they have been hurt by parents who have not spent "quality time" with them. Their parents may be around, but they are so absorbed in other concerns that they are not present to their children, and this causes them to suffer. There is no doubt that if we give God our time, we will be able to find time for others, too. By paying attention to God, we learn to pay attention to others.

Thus we must count on Jesus' promise: "Truly, I tell you, there is no one who has left house or brothers or sisters or mother or father or children or fields, for my sake and for the sake of the good news, who will not receive a hundredfold now in this age—houses, brothers and sisters, mothers and children, and fields..." (Mk 10:29). In contemporary terms, we could say that the person who turns the television off for fifteen minutes to pray will receive a hundredfold in this life; his or her time will multiply a hundredfold, perhaps not in the number of minutes but, surely, in the quality of the minutes spent. Prayer gives us the grace to live each moment of life with greater fruitfulness.

Time dedicated to God does not deprive others

We must be firmly convinced that the time we give to God is never time taken away from those who need our love and presence. This idea springs from a false

sense of guilt founded on a mistaken sense of charity. As noted earlier, fidelity to times of prayer guar-
antees that we will be able to be present to others and
to sincerely love them. Experience shows that truly
prayerful individuals are also more attentive, delicate,
impartial, and sensitive toward the sufferings of others and are better able to comfort and console them.
Prayer makes us better persons—and no one would
hold that against us!

Concerning the relationship between prayer life
and charity toward others, numerous misunderstand-
ings have led many Christians to turn away from contemplation, with disastrous consequences. While
much may be said in this regard, let us simply look at
the words of St. John of the Cross to clarify the matter and emphasize the legitimate right Christians have
to set aside time for prayer.

> Let those who go bustling about, who think
> they can transform the world with their exterior
> works and preaching, take note that they would
> profit the Church more and be far more pleas-
> ing to God (not to mention the good example
> they would give) if they spent half as much time
> abiding with God in prayer, even though their
> souls would not be as advanced as the person
> inclined to pray. Certainly, they would accom-
> plish more and with less toil with one work than

they would now with a thousand works thanks
to their prayers and the increased spiritual
strength from which they would benefit.
Otherwise, their lives would be reduced to making a lot of noise and accomplishing little more
than nothing, if not nothing at all, or indeed at
times even doing harm. May God forbid that
the salt should begin to lose its taste, since, even
if it seems to produce some effect, in reality it
would be good for nothing, for it is certain that
good works cannot be accomplished save with
the grace of God. Oh, how much could be written here about this matter![3]

Is it enough to pray while working?

Some people will say, "I don't have time to pray, but
I try to think about God as much as I can while I go
about my tasks. I offer him my work and I think that
kind of prayer suffices."

They are not completely wrong. A man or woman
can remain intimately united with God in the midst of
their activities in a way that this constitutes their
prayer life. The Lord can grant this grace to those
who have no other alternative. Obviously, the ideal is
to raise our minds to God as frequently as possible

---

3. This passage was translated directly from the Spanish edition,
Obras Completas of St. John of the Cross (Burgos, Spain: Editorial
Monte Carmelo, 1997); see *Cántico Espiritual,* Canción 28, p. 871.

amidst our daily tasks, because work done and offered to God is a form of prayer.

Nevertheless, we should be realistic. It is not that easy to remain united with God as we go about our workaday concerns. Our natural tendency is to become completely caught up in what we are doing. Moreover, if we do not know how to take an occasional pause in order to engage ourselves solely with God, then it will be hard to keep God's presence in mind while working. We must re-educate the heart, and the surest means for this is fidelity to prayer.

The same thing is true in personal relationships. It would be an illusion for a man to think that he loves his wife and children if he is so engrossed in his work that he cannot dedicate even a few minutes to them, or to be there for them 100 percent. Love quickly suffocates when one does not make time for it. On the other hand, love expands and breathes in gratuitous freedom. We should learn how to "waste time" for the sake of others. In this sense, we gain more than we lose. This is one way of understanding the Gospel passage about losing one's life in order to find it.

If we concern ourselves with God, God concerns himself with our affairs—and in a far better way than we ever could. Let us humbly acknowledge our

natural inclination to become obsessed or excessive-
ly absorbed with our activities. We will only be healed
of this ailment if, with prudence, we know how to
regularly set aside our concerns, even if they seem
urgent or important, in order to generously give our
time to God.

The pitfall of false sincerity

In an age imbued with the idea that "freedom"
means "being yourself," there is another frequent
objection that can hinder our fidelity: "I find prayer
pleasing, but only when I want to pray. To pray when
I don't feel like it would be forced and fake. It would
be insincere, even hypocritical. I will pray when the
desire comes to me...."

We must respond to this objection by saying that
if we wait until the desire to pray wells up within us,
we might wait until the end of our life. Desire is a
beautiful but changeable motivation. There is an
equally legitimate, but deeper and more constant reason to seek God in prayer: God invites us to pray. In
the Gospel, Jesus asks us "to pray always and not to
lose heart" (Lk 18:1). Faith should guide us rather
than our state of mind.

The above-mentioned notions of freedom and
spontaneity, so appealing today, are, at best, misleading.
True freedom lies not in allowing ourselves to be

swayed by the impulse of the moment, but in refusing to be imprisoned by our emotional ups and downs, to base our decisions on the fundamental choices we have made that do not alter with changing circumstances.

Freedom is the capacity to be guided by what is true and not by external realities. We must be humble enough to acknowledge that we can be shallow and fickle. What charmed me yesterday may become intolerable tomorrow because of a change in mood or weather. Today we are indifferent toward something that we wanted intensely yesterday. If we make decisions based on desires, we become tragic prisoners of ourselves, of our most superficial moods and feelings.

Let us not deceive ourselves regarding authenticity. What is authentic love? Love that varies day by day, depending on the mood of the moment, or love that is constant and faithful to its promises?

Fidelity to prayer is a school of freedom where we learn to be sincere in love because we gradually learn to ground our relationship with God not on unsteady impressions or shifts in mood, but on the cornerstone of faith. Then the foundation of our fidelity to God is as solid and steadfast as a rock. "Jesus Christ is the same yesterday and today and forever" (Heb 13:8), and "his mercy is...from generation to generation" (Lk 1:50). If we persevere in this school, then we will see how our superficial and shifting relationships become more stable, more profound, more faithful, and, therefore, happier.

It is perfectly legitimate for the human person to shun constraints on his or her spontaneity. God did not make us to be at permanent odds with ourselves, to act contrary to our nature, but this happens because of the internal rift caused by sin.

Yet, the human desire for freedom cannot be truly realized through unfettered inclinations. This could be damaging to us since pure spontaneity is not always oriented toward the good. Rather, human spontaneity must undergo deep purification and healing, because our nature is wounded; that is, we experience disharmony and imbalance between what we naturally desire and that for which we are truly made, between our feelings and God's will to which we must remain faithful and which is our true goal and authentic good.

Thus, we can only truly fulfill our desire to be free to the extent that we allow divine grace to heal us; and prayer plays a very important role in the healing process. This can also happen in the midst of trials and purification—the "dark night," which St. John of the Cross explained accurately. Once the dark night ends, and our tendencies are properly ordered, we become truly free: we love and naturally desire what is good for us, which is, ultimately, what God wants for us. Thus, we can be "spontaneous," because our inclinations have been harmonized with divine wisdom. We can then "obey" our nature, now restored in grace. Of course, we cannot fully achieve such harmony in this life, but only in the Kingdom, which explains why we must still resist some of our tendencies. Nevertheless, in this life, those who pray become increasingly capable of loving and spontaneously doing good, which initially required great effort. Thanks to the action of the Holy Spirit, it becomes easier and more natural to practice virtue. As St. Paul wrote, "Where the Spirit of the Lord is, there lies freedom" (2 Cor 3:17).

The trap of false humility

The false reasoning we have just considered sometimes assumes a subtler form. St. Teresa of Avila almost fell into the trap of abandoning prayer (a possibility that could have caused terrible damage to the Church!). In fact, one of her main reasons for writing her autobiography was to warn against this trap.

St. Teresa of Avila describes this temptation as a card that the devil plays most skillfully. It is a temptation that brings beginners in prayer to see their

faults, infidelities, and lack of conversion, thus induc-
ing them to abandon prayer. One can think: "I am so
full of defects. I am not advancing. I cannot be con-
verted. I cannot love the Lord seriously enough. It is
sheer hypocrisy to stand before him like this. I am
making a mockery of holiness. I am no better than
those who never pray. It would be more honest to
stop praying altogether!"

In her autobiography, St. Teresa writes of a similar temptation that she experienced after some
years of assiduous prayer. She abandoned prayer
for a year, until she met a Dominican priest who
led her back to it. At that time, St. Teresa was living in the convent of the Incarnation in Avila and
had a great desire to give herself to God and
prayer. However, she was far from being a saint!
Though she realized Jesus was asking her to abandon her custom of frequenting the convent's visit-
ing room, she could not detach herself from that
habit. Gregarious and charming by nature, she
enjoyed the company of the society that usually
met at the convent. While she was not doing anything seriously wrong, Jesus was calling her elsewhere. Her periods of prayer were a veritable martyrdom: in God's presence, she was aware of her
infidelity, but did not possess the strength to leave

everything for his sake. In addition, this torment was leading her to abandon prayer. "I am not worthy to present myself before the Lord; as I am unable to give everything to him, it is a mockery; I would do better to stop praying...."

St. Teresa calls this temptation "false humility." She had finally abandoned prayer when her confessor made her realize that, in doing so, she was losing all possibility of becoming better one day. Rather than abandon prayer, she had to persevere in it in order to obtain, in due time, the grace of total conversion and fuller self-giving to the Lord.

This is a very important point. We are not saints when we begin our prayer life, and this becomes increasingly clear to us as we continue down the path. Those who do not face God in the silence of prayer do not realize their infidelities and defects. On the other hand, these are so evident to those who pray that this can cause great grief and the temptation to cease praying. We cannot despair but carry on, certain that perseverance will obtain the grace of conversion. No matter how serious the sin committed, we must never make it an excuse to abandon prayer, despite the suggestions or insinuations that proceed from the devil or from our own conscience. The more miserable we are the more reason for us to

pray. Who will cure us of our infidelities and sins
except the merciful Lord? Where will we find health
of soul if not in humble and persevering prayer?
"Those who are well have no need of a physician,
but those who are sick" (Mt 9:12). The more sin
causes the soul to fall ill, the more reason to pray.
The more injured we are, the more right we have to
seek refuge in the heart of Jesus, who alone can heal
us. If we turn away from him because of our sins,
then where will we find healing and pardon? If we
wait until we are upright and holy to pray, then we
will wait a very long time. This attitude only shows a
poor understanding of the Gospel. It may seem to be
humility, but, in reality, we have become presumptu-
ous and distrustful of God.

It can happen that after falling into sin, we
become ashamed and unhappy with ourselves and,
even if we do not completely abandon prayer, we let
some time pass before going back to it, allowing the
painful wound on our conscience to ease a bit. This
is a very serious mistake, greater than the sin previ-
ously committed, for this means that we do not
trust God's mercy and are ignorant of his love. This
grieves God more than the thousands of other
foolish things we could have done. St. Thérèse of
Lisieux, who possessed a profound understanding

of God, said that what grieves God's heart the most is our lack of confidence in him.

Contrary to our initial impulse and justified attitude—"just" in the biblical sense of being in harmony with God's revealed mystery—the sinner must immediately throw herself or himself into God's merciful arms, humble, repentant and trusting that she or he is welcome and forgiven.

Once we have asked God's pardon, we should not hesitate to return to our usual pious practices, especially that of prayer. If called for, we receive the sacrament of Reconciliation, but, meanwhile, continue the habit of praying. This is the best way to avoid sin because it is what gives the greatest honor to God's mercy.

In a beautiful consideration, St. Teresa of Avila says that the person who prays will keep on falling, because he has many shortcomings and weaknesses, but because he prays, each fall will help him leap higher. God makes everything, including one's faults, work for the well being and progress of the one who is faithful to prayer.

> I repeat that no one who has begun to practice prayer should be discouraged and say: "If I am going to fall again, it would be better not to go on

practicing prayer." I think this is true if such a person gives up prayer and does not amend his evil life; but if he does not give up, he may have confidence that prayer will bring him into the haven of light. This was a matter about which the devil kept plaguing me, and I suffered so much through thinking myself lacking in humility for continuing to pray when I was so wicked that, as I have said, for a year and a half I gave it up—or at any rate for a year; I am not quite sure about the six months. This would have been nothing less than plunging into hell—nor was it; there was no need for any devils to send me there. Oh, God help me, how terribly blind I was! How well the devil succeeds in his purpose when he pursues us like this! The deceiver knows that if a soul perseveres in practicing prayer, it will be lost to him, and that by God's goodness all the relapses into which [the devil] can lead it will only help [the soul] to make greater strides in God's service. And this is a matter of some concern to the devil.[4]

Giving Oneself Completely to God

The moment has come to consider the close ties between the life of prayer and other aspects of Christian life. In other words, the advancement and

---

4. St. Teresa of Avila, *Autobiography of St. Teresa of Avila,* trans. and ed. by E. Allison Peers (New York: Image, 1960), chap. 19.

deepening of one's prayer life are seen not during prayer, but in what we do outside of it. Progress in prayer is essentially progress in love and purity of heart; and true love is seen more in action.

For example, it would be completely illusory for us to try to progress in prayer if our whole life is not marked by a deep and sincere desire to give ourselves completely to God and to conform our lives in the fullest way possible with his will. Without this, the life of piety would soon reach a dead end. God gives himself completely to us (the goal of prayer) only when we give ourselves completely to him. The one who does not give everything will not possess everything. To hold something back—such as a small defect we refuse to correct, a grudge, or a deliberate act of disobedience—not wanting to abandon it into God's hands, will make the life of prayer sterile.

With malicious intent, a few nuns once asked St. John of the Cross: "What should we do to enter into ecstasy?" In his response, the saint presented the etymological meaning of the word. He said that the nuns should renounce their will and do God's will, since ecstasy is nothing other than a "going out" of oneself and remaining in an enraptured state before God. This happens when we obey, because we leave behind our will and self in order to be united to God.

To give ourselves to God, we must be detached from ourselves. Love is ecstatic by nature. When love is strong, it dwells on the lover more than the lover dwells on himself. How can we experience the ecstasy of love in prayer when all we do is to seek ourselves or are too attached to material things, comfort, and well being, when we are incapable of bearing the smallest setback? How will we be able to love God if we cannot forget ourselves for the sake of our brothers and sisters?

We should strike a balance in the spiritual life, and this is not always easy. On one hand, we must accept our misery and not wait to be holy in order to begin praying. On the other hand, however, we must aspire to perfection. Without the deep and constant desire to be holy, even with a keen awareness that we can achieve nothing on our own and that only God can make us holy, prayer will always be a superficial exercise producing scant fruit. It is proper to the nature of love to reach out to the Absolute, that is, to give oneself to the point of folly.

We must also be aware that certain lifestyles either facilitate or hinder prayer. How can we be recollected when we are distracted by a thousand superficial concerns throughout the day, or thoughtlessly involve ourselves in useless conversations and vain curiosity? Or when we do not guard the heart, the eyes, and the mind, through which we all too readily escape from the Essential One?

Certainly, we cannot live without some distractions, without some moments of leisure. However, what is important is to know how always to return to God, who makes us steadfast and able to live united to him.

We should also realize that we achieve more progress in our prayer when we endeavor to face any circumstance with complete abandonment and serene confidence in God, living the moment without tormenting ourselves with worries about tomorrow, and trying to complete each task without becoming anxious about the next. Again, this is not easy, but it is very advantageous to acquire this attitude as much as possible.[5]

It is also important to live continually under God's gaze, in his presence, in constant dialogue with him, remembering God as often as we can in the midst of our tasks, and dealing with any situation with God by our side. The more effort we make in this regard, the easier prayer becomes. In the process, if we do not stray from God, we will find God more easily! Prayer

---

5. See *Recherche la paix et poursuis-la. Petit traité sur la paix du coeur,* Editions du Lion de Juda.

thus becomes, as it should, a continuous union, not necessarily in the sense of explicit prayer, but of a habit of living in God's presence. All too often, we view ourselves with complacency or self-critical scrutiny; we are afraid of how others see us, wishing to avoid their judgment or desirous of their admiration. We will only achieve interior freedom when we have learned to live under the Lord's loving and merciful gaze.

Brother Lawrence of the Resurrection, a seventeenth-century Carmelite friar, offers valuable advice on this matter. As a cook at the monastery, he learned to live in profound union with God amid the most engrossing activities. (See Appendix II, page 123.)

There remains much to say about the inseparable bond between prayer and other aspects of the spiritual life. One of the best sources [on this topic] is the writings of the saints, especially those whom the Church has recognized as having a special grace to teach about the spiritual life, including Teresa of Avila, John of the Cross, Francis de Sales, and Thérèse of Lisieux among others.

All we have considered so far are aids to overcoming obstacles to prayer and are indispensable if we are to be sincere in prayer and thus make progress. Moreover, if we understand these teachings, many false problems concerning how to pray well will disappear by themselves.

The attitudes that have been described are not founded on human wisdom but on the Gospel. These attitudes are faith, trusting abandonment into God's hands, poverty in spirit, and childlike spirituality. As the reader will have already noted, these attitudes must be the basis not only of our prayer life, but also of our entire existence. The close relationship between prayer and life as a whole becomes apparent. Prayer is a school where we learn and practice certain attitudes toward God, toward ourselves, and toward the world, which become the foundation of our being and acting. Prayer creates a "quality" or "mark" within us that we maintain and leave in everything we do, and it bestows on us peace, inner freedom, and a genuine love for God and neighbor. Prayer is a school of love because all the virtues we exercise in its practice allow love to grow in our hearts. Here lies prayer's vital importance.

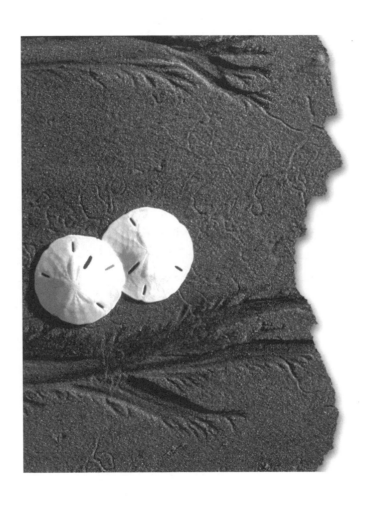

CHAPTER TWO

MAKING TIMES OF PRAYER MEANINGFUL

When we have decided to dedicate time to prayer each day, what, we may ask, is the best way to spend that time? There is no one answer.

In the first place, we are all very different. There are as many differences between people as there are faces. Each person's relationship with God is unique, and so too is his or her prayer. There is no single path or method for everyone; this would violate the freedom and diversity of spiritual journeys. Every believer must discover, under the guidance and action of the Holy Spirit, the ways in which God wishes to lead him or her.

In the second place, we must realize that our prayer life evolves and has stages of development. What is useful at one point in our spiritual journey

will not be in another. Our approach to prayer can
vary, depending on whether we are at the beginning
of our journey or if the Lord has initiated us into a
particular spiritual state or "castle," as St. Teresa of
Avila would describe it. Sometimes we will give, while
at other times we will receive. Sometimes we will rest
and other times we will have to struggle.

Ultimately, an experience of prayer is difficult to
describe because it often transcends the conscious
awareness of the person praying. The experience
concerns intimate, mysterious realities which are
beyond human language; words fail to express what
takes place between God and a soul.

Let us add that those who speak of the prayer life
do so through their own experience or through what
others have confided to them, and this is very limited
considering the wealth and diversity of experiences.

Despite these obstacles, I address the topic with
the simple hope that the Lord will allow me to offer
some guidelines, which are in no way comprehensive
and infallible, but which may be a source of light and
encouragement to the reader of good will.

HOW TO SPEND TIME IN PRAYER

How ought we to spend a period of prayer? Before
answering, we must note that there are times when
there is no need to raise this question.

When prayer flows from the source, so to speak, that is, when loving communication with God takes place, we have no need to wonder how to structure prayer time. In fact, this is what should happen, because, according to St. Teresa of Avila, prayer is "to realize how much it means to you to have God's friendship and how much he loves you."[6] Two people who love each other deeply hardly have problems thinking of how to spend their time together. It is enough to be together as often as they can! Unfortunately, we have not reached this point because our love for God is weak.

Prayer that flows easily of itself as communication with God is a gift we need only receive. It is diverse by its nature and is found at different stages and in varying degrees along the spiritual path.

For example, new converts, sincerely enthused by their recent discovery of God, are full of the joy and fervor of neophytes. They have no problems in prayer because they feel drawn along by grace, happy to consecrate time to Jesus, and having a thousand and one things to say and to ask of him. They are full of loving sentiments and consoling thoughts.

May such persons enjoy those moments of grace without worry and be thankful to the Lord for them.

---

6. St. Teresa of Avila, *Autobiography*, chap. 8.

But they should also remain humble and take care to neither think themselves saints because of those feelings of fervor nor judge others who show less zeal! The grace of the first moments of conversion has not eliminated faults or imperfections; it has merely masked them. Therefore, such individuals should not be surprised when, one fine day, their fervor ebbs and their imperfections, which supposedly "disappeared" thanks to their conversion, suddenly reappear with unexpected violence. May they then persevere and learn how to benefit from their aridity and trials as they learned to benefit from the time of blessing.

The question of how to use the time of prayer is also not raised by those at the other end of the spiritual journey: those who are grasped by God and cannot resist or do anything on their own. They are immobilized and they can only surrender and consent to the presence of God, who permeates them completely. They can only say "yes"; however, they must entrust themselves to a spiritual director who can confirm the authenticity of the graces received, for this is unusual, and it is, therefore, advisable to openly confide in another. When extraordinary graces in prayer cease, uncertainties concerning the cause can lead to doubts and struggles. Souls that are open to another's direction receive reassurance regarding the divine origin of these graces and are capable of embracing them fully.

Let us now consider the more common intermediate case. It is helpful for us to do so because at times the initial manifestation is imperceptible, causing doubts and even scruples regarding the course of action to take. In this case, persons do not know if they are doing the right thing, but they have no choice. In this situation the Holy Spirit steers them toward a more passive prayer—after a long time of "active" prayer—consisting principally in interior dialogue with Jesus and voluntary acts of self-giving, reflection, and meditation.

~~Then, one fine day, they find their manner of praying transformed. They find it hard to meditate and to engage in conversation with God. They suffer aridity and feel inclined to remain before the Lord without saying anything or thinking about anything specific, but in a quiet attitude of full, serene, and loving attention toward God.~~ This loving attitude, which proceeds more from the heart than the mind, is almost imperceptible, but can become more intense later, like a fire of love rising from a small spark. Moreover, when these souls try to act another way, that is, to revive their active prayer, they fail. There are times when they may experience scruples because of their impression of being inactive.

Now, when souls find themselves in this state, they should remain there without becoming restless or anxious. God wants to bring them to a more profound prayer, and this is a very great grace. These souls must allow themselves to be moved by God and follow their inclination to remain passive. It is enough for them to seek to be led serenely toward God. This is not the moment for them to take action, by virtue of their faculties or capacities; it is the moment to allow God to act.

Let us note that this state is not the total grasp of God as discussed earlier. The intelligence and imagination continue to engage in some activity: thoughts and images come and go, but at a superficial level, without the person paying attention to them, as they are involuntary. More important than the mental agitation, which is inevitable, is the heart's profound turning toward God.

In the above situations, we do not have to consider how we are to spend our time in prayer because the answer is already given. But the question remains for those who have good will, but who are not yet set aflame by God's love. They have not yet received the grace of passive prayer, understand that prayer is important and therefore want to pray regularly, but do not know how to go about it. What advice can we give to these persons? ~~One cannot answer, "Do this or that," or, "Pray this way or that."~~ Rather, it seems more prudent to offer the ~~basic principles that should guide a soul at prayer.~~

We have already described the basic attitudes guiding the soul when it prays and which are applicable to any form of prayer and to a Christian's existence as a whole. ~~We wish to repeat that what counts, above all, is not the formula or the "how" of prayer, but the climate and the state of mind and heart with which one approaches prayer and upon which depend one's perseverance and fruitfulness.~~

Here are some general guidelines that offer a kind of interior landscape with signposts along the way. A person who wants to pray may freely travel according to his or her present level of spirituality and the impulses of the Holy Spirit. ~~Familiarity with these signposts equips the faithful to find his or her way and so discover what must be done in prayer.~~

This interior landscape of the Christian's prayer life is in some way defined by and modeled upon certain theological truths.

THE PRIMACY OF DIVINE ACTION

The first principle is simple but very important. ~~What matters in prayer is not what we do, but what God does in us during those moments.~~

This principle is liberating because sometimes we find ourselves incapable of doing anything in prayer, which is not at all tragic, because if we cannot act, then God can act—and always does—in a more profound way in our hearts, even without our being aware of it. In the final analysis, the essential act in prayer is to place ourselves in God's presence and to remain there. Now, God is not the God of the dead, but of the living. This presence of the living God is active, vivifying. It heals and sanctifies us. We cannot sit before a fire without becoming warm; we cannot be out in the sun without tanning—from the moment we settle ourselves and remain facing a certain direction.

Similarly, if our prayer consists simply in standing before God without doing anything, without thinking of anything specific or feeling anything in particular, but with an attitude of profound readiness and trusting abandonment, then we allow God to act in the secret of our heart. Nothing else matters, and we could do nothing better.

It would be a mistake to measure the value of our prayer by what we accomplished during that time. We would then believe everything depended on the good and useful things we had thought or done, and thus become disheartened when we fail in this regard. Our prayer may seem miserable, but God secretly works wonders in our souls, the fruits of which we shall only see much later. The tremendous blessings that come from prayer are not the fruit of our thoughts or actions, but of the often secret and invisible work of God in our hearts. We will only see the results of our prayer in the Kingdom!

St. Thérèse of Lisieux was very aware of this. She had the problem of falling asleep while praying! This was not her fault, for having entered Carmel at a very young age, she lacked sufficient sleep. Her weakness, however, did not sadden her.

> I believe that young children are as pleasing to their parents when they are asleep as when they are awake. Moreover, physicians are obliged to put their patients to sleep before operating on them. The Lord sees our frailty and remembers that we are only dust.[7]

The passive aspect of prayer is most important. It is less concerned with doing things than being open to God's action. Sometimes we must prepare for and assist God's action with our own; however, more often we need only consent to these actions, and this is when the more important things happen. It may even be necessary for us to suspend all action so that

---

7. Cf. St. Thérèse of Lisieux, *The Story of a Soul,* trans. John Beevers (Manila: Sinag-tala, 1987).

God may freely act in us. It is this, as so well illustrated by St. John of the Cross, which explains times of aridity, certain moments when the intelligence or the imagination do not function during prayer, and when we experience the impossibility of meditating or feeling anything at all. God allows this aridity, this "dark night," so that he alone may work on us in a profound way, just as a doctor anesthetizes a patient so that he may do his job tranquilly!

We will return to this theme, but let us keep in mind that if, despite our good will, we are unable to pray well and remain unmoved and incapable of beautiful thoughts, we should not become sad. Rather, let us offer up our poverty to God's action and our prayer will be more valuable than if we satisfied ourselves! St. Francis de Sales says, "Lord, I am no more than a dry log; set me afire!"

THE PRIMACY OF LOVE

The second fundamental principle is *the primacy of love above everything else.* St. Teresa of Avila says that in prayer what matters is not to think much but to love much. This is also a liberating consideration. If we cannot think, meditate, or feel anything, we can always love. If we are at the point of exhaustion, oppressed by distractions, and unable to pray, we can offer this to the Lord with serene confidence. In this way, we love and offer a magnificent prayer. Love is king, regardless of the circumstances, and everything always flows from it. Quoting St. John of the Cross, St. Thérèse of Lisieux would say, "Love profits from everything, from good as well as bad." Love profits from feelings as well as dryness, from inspirations as well as aridity, from virtue as well as sin.

This principle is united with the primacy of God's action over ours. In prayer, our principal task is to love, but in relation to God to love is, in the first place, allowing ourselves *to be loved*. This is not as easy as it seems! We must believe in love even when we have the tendency to doubt it. We must also accept our misery.

It is often easier to love than to allow ourselves to be loved. It is gratifying to reach out to others, to give, and to believe ourselves useful! Instead, allowing ourselves to be loved presupposes that we accept to do nothing, to be nothing. This is the first task of prayer: not to think, offer, or do anything for God, but to allow God to love us as little children, to give God the joy of loving us. This is hard because it supposes that we have unshakable faith in God's love for us. It also implies that we accept our poverty. This is a fundamental point: there is no authentic love for God that is not based on the recognition of the absolute priority of his love for us, and the understanding that before doing anything, we should learn to receive. In his first letter, St. John writes: "In this is love, not that we loved God but that he loved us" (1 Jn 4:10).

As regards God, the first act of love, the foundation of any act of love, is this: to believe that we are loved, to allow ourselves to be loved in our poverty, just as we are, regardless of our merits and virtues. If this is the foundation of our relationship with God, then we are on the right path. We will always fall into a kind of hypocrisy if we, and not God, occupy the first place, the center of our lives, our actions, and even of our virtues.

This point of view is very demanding. It requires decentralization, a great self-forgetfulness that is at the same time liberating. God does not await certain works, acts, or achievements from us. We are, after all, useless servants. "God does not need our works, but he thirsts for our love," says St. Thérèse of Lisieux. First, God asks us to allow ourselves to be loved, to believe in his love, and this is always possible. Prayer is fundamentally this: to place ourselves in God's presence and to allow him to love us. Love's response comes during or outside of prayer. If we allow ourselves to be loved, then God will personally work the good in us and give us the grace to carry out good works: "For we are what he has made us, created in Christ Jesus for good works, which God prepared beforehand to be our way of life" (Eph 2:10).

It follows that all we have to do in prayer is to seek love and to strengthen it. This is the only criterion for judging whether we are doing badly or well in prayer. Everything that inspires us to love is good. Of course, true love is not superficial or sentimental, even though ardent feelings have their value when God grants them to us.

Everything that nourishes our love for God is beneficial for our prayer. Whatever makes us grow in gratitude and confidence in God awakens or stimulates the desire for self-giving, of belonging to him, and of serving him faithfully, which should become a habitual part of our prayer.

Seek to be simple

In prayer, we must not ramble on or multiply thoughts and considerations that end up taking us away from true conversion of heart. What use are elevated and varied thoughts about the mysteries of the faith? What benefit is drawn from constantly changing the subject of meditation, or exploring the theological truths and Scripture passages if they do not lead to the firm resolution to give oneself to God and to renounce oneself for love of him? St. Thérèse of Lisieux says that to love is to give everything and to give one's self. If our daily prayers steadily revolve around and return to one idea: stirring our hearts into giving ourselves totally to the Lord, to be persistent in serving him, then such prayer would seem poorer and yet be better!

As regards the primacy of love, we have this example from St. Thérèse of Lisieux. Before she died, her sister, Sister Agnes, asked Thérèse, "What are you thinking about?" She answered, "I am not thinking about anything. I cannot think, I am suffering too much, and so I am praying." "And what do you tell Jesus?" "I don't tell him anything. I love him!"

This is the poorest yet the most profound of prayers: a simple act of love beyond words or ideas. We must seek to be simple. Ultimately, our prayers need not be more than this: no words, no ideas, not a succession of particular unique acts, but a single, simple act of love! We need time and the profound work of grace to acquire such simplicity, because sin has made us so complicated and fragmented. We should at least remember that the value of prayer is not measured by the abundance and variety of actions, but by making a simple act of love. The further we advance in the interior life, the simpler our prayer becomes.

Be warned of a temptation that may arise during prayer. Beautiful and profound thoughts and insights can occur to us while praying. They can come as illuminations regarding God's mystery or heartening insights about our life. These thoughts or inspirations, which may seem ingenious, can be a trap that we must guard against. Of course, God does grant us lights and inspirations during prayer, but we should realize that such thoughts can take us away from God's true presence. We can be carried away or exult in these inspirations, and we end up cultivating them to the point that we focus on them more than on God. Then, when our prayer ends, we realize that these were nothing great and rather futile.

GOD GIVES HIMSELF
THROUGH THE HUMANITY OF JESUS

A third fundamental principle that sustains the contemplative life of a Christian is *our encounter with God in the humanity of Jesus Christ.*

We pray in order to enter into communion with God, but no one has ever seen or met God. What, then, is the way, the means given to us to find God? The only Mediator, Jesus Christ, true God and true Man. The humanity of Jesus, God the Son made man, is the surest and most available point of encounter

with God. As St. Paul says, "For in him the whole full-
ness of deity dwells bodily" (Col 2:9). The humanity
of Jesus is the primordial sacrament through which
the Divinity makes himself accessible to men.

As persons of flesh and bone, we need tangible
helps in order to accede to spiritual realities. We need
to see, touch, and feel things. God knows this, which
is why the mystery of the Incarnation took place.
Jesus' concrete and perceivable humanity is for us the
expression of the marvelous humbling of God. God
knows of what we are made and he offers us the possibility of reaching out and touching the Divine with
our human hands. The spirit has become flesh. Jesus
is our way to God: "Philip said to him, 'Lord, show
us the Father, and we will be satisfied.' Jesus said to
him, 'Have I been with you all this time, Philip, and
you still do not know me? Whoever has seen me has
seen the Father'" (Jn 14:8–9).

There is something very beautiful and mysterious
here. In all its aspects, the humanity of Jesus, even
the most humble and secondary in appearances, is
like an *immense space of communion with God.* Every time
we receive him in faith, we are "in touch" with the
Father through every aspect of Christ's humanity—
each feature, even the smallest and the most hidden,
each word, action, and gesture, and each phase of his

life, from his conception in Mary's womb to the Ascension. As we go through Christ's humanity, like a scene in which we take part or a book written for us, we make it our very own in faith and love. We do not stop growing in communion with the unreachable and unfathomable mystery of God.

This means that a Christian's prayer is always based on his or her relationship with the Savior's humanity.[8] All the various forms of Christian prayer (we shall give more examples later) are theologically justified and have, as a common denominator, contact with God through a specific aspect of Jesus' humanity. In order to achieve communion with God, it suffices to be united through faith to this humanity, which is the effective sign of humanity's union with God.

Bérulle beautifully expounds on how the mysteries of Jesus' life, occurring long ago, remain living and vivifying realities for those who contemplate them with the eyes of faith. We must raise the question of the perpetuity of these mysteries. They did in fact happen in the past, but they are present with a strength and vigor that does not wane. Neither does

---

8. St. Teresa of Avila insisted upon this truth, contrary to everything taught during her time, when pure contemplation was thought of as achieving union with God by abandoning, at a certain point, all sensible references, including the humanity of the Lord. Cf. St. Teresa of Avila, *Autobiography*, chap. 22.

the love with which they were realized fade. The spirit, the state, the vigor, the merit of each mystery is therefore always present. This obliges us to deal with the mysteries of Jesus not as things long past and dead, but as alive and present and from which we too can gather fruit in the present and in eternity.

Applying this thought to Jesus' infancy, Bérulle says that Jesus experienced childhood, but the circumstances of that childhood have passed and he is no longer a child. But there is something divine in this mystery, which endures in heaven and produces in souls similar grace, which Jesus is pleased to give in this first and humble stage of his life.

There are a thousand ways of touching the humanity of Jesus: contemplating his works and gestures; meditating upon and remembering his behavior, his words, and each event of his life on earth; gazing on Christ's face in an icon; adoring his body in the Eucharist; saying his name lovingly and keeping it in our hearts. These will help us to pray if they are done not for the sake of intellectual curiosity, but because we lovingly seek him: "I sought him whom my soul loves" (Song 3:1).

In this way, we make the humanity of Jesus our own and, through it, embark on true communication with the unfathomable mystery of God. This is not mere intellectual speculation but faith—faith as a theological virtue, faith enlivened by love. St. John of the Cross insisted that faith alone has the power and strength needed to make us truly possess the mystery of God through the person of Jesus Christ. Only faith allows us to truly reach God in the depths of his mystery; faith, which is to hold fast with our entire being to Christ, in whom God gives himself to us.

The consequence of all this, as we have seen, is that Christians pray by communing with the humanity of Jesus—in thoughts, glances, and acts of the will—with each person observing what he or she deems most suitable among the diverse "methods of prayer."

St. Teresa of Avila recommends this classic way (at least in the Western Church), of entering prayer: live alongside Jesus as a friend who listens to you and engages you in a lively conversation.

> We can imagine ourselves in the presence of Christ, and accustom ourselves to being enkindled with great love for his sacred humanity, live in his presence, and speak with him, ask him for the things we need, complain to him of trials, rejoice with him in joys, yet never allow joys to make us forgetful of him. We have no need of set prayers, but can just use such words as suit our desires and needs. This is an excellent way of making progress and of making it very quickly;

and those who strive always to have this precious companionship, make good use of it, and really learn to love this Lord to whom we owe so much, have, I think, achieved a definite gain.[9]

God Dwells in Our Hearts

We would now like to mention a fourth theological principle of great importance as a guide in the life of prayer. By it, *we try to place ourselves in God's presence.* Now, there are as many ways of living in God's presence as there are diverse manners of praying. God is present in creation and we may contemplate him there; he is present in the Eucharist and we can adore him there; he is present in the Word and we can find him as we meditate on Sacred Scripture. However, God is also present in another important way: God is present in our hearts.

As in the other forms of God's presence, his presence in our hearts is not, strictly speaking, something experienced, even if this is gradually possible at certain privileged moments. God's presence in our hearts is a matter of faith. Regardless of our feelings, we know through faith or sure knowledge that God dwells deep in our hearts. "Or do you not know that your body is a temple of the Holy Spirit within you,

---

9. St. Teresa of Avila, *Autobiography*, chap. 12.

which you have from God, and that you are not your own?" (1 Cor 6:19)

St. Teresa of Avila tells us that understanding this truth was a light that profoundly transformed her prayer life.

> I think that if I had understood then, as I do now, how such a great King really dwells within this little palace of my soul, I would not have left him alone so often, but would have stayed with him and never have allowed his dwelling-place to get so dirty. How wonderful it is to think that the One whose greatness could fill a thousand worlds, and very many more, confines himself within so small a space, just as he was pleased to dwell within the womb of his most holy Mother! Being the Lord, he has, of course, perfect freedom, and as he loves us, he fashions himself to our measure.[10]

This is the authentic meaning of recollection or the withdrawing into the inner self which happens in prayer. Otherwise, recollection would be a mere "closing in" on one's self. Nevertheless, the Christian legitimately enters into himself or herself when God dwells there in a way deeper than all interior miseries and despite all miseries put together. As St. Augustine says, God is more intimate to us than we

---

10. St. Teresa of Avila, *The Way of Perfection,* chap. 28.

are to ourselves. Or as St. John of the Cross says, "God, who dwells in us by the grace of the Holy Spirit, is at the innermost core of our soul."

In this truth we see all forms of prayer as a "supplication of the heart." Entering with faith into our hearts, we unite ourselves with God who dwells in us. If prayer unites us with God as "Other"—"outside" us and eminently present in the humanity of Jesus— then it is through this inner presence that we can enter our hearts to find Jesus, so close and within our reach. " 'Who will go up to heaven for us, and get it for us so that we may hear it and observe it?' Neither is it beyond the sea, that you should say, 'Who will cross to the other side of the sea for us, and get it for us so that we may hear it and observe it?' No, the word is very near to you; it is in your mouths and in your heart for you to observe" (Dt 30:12–14).

> Do you suppose it is of little importance for a distracted soul to understand this truth, to find that in order to speak to its Eternal Father and to take its delight in him it has no need to go to heaven or to speak in a loud voice? However quietly we speak, God is so near that he will hear us; we need no wings to go in search of him, but have only to find a place where we can be alone and look upon him present within us. Nor need we feel strange in the presence of so kind a Guest; in great humility

we should speak to him as to a father, asking him
for those things we would ask of a father, telling
him our troubles, begging him to put them right,
and yet realizing that we are not worthy to be
called his children.[11]

When we do not know how to pray, it is very simple to proceed in this way: let us recollect ourselves.
Let us be silent and enter our hearts, descend into
our interior selves, reunite ourselves with that presence of Jesus who lives in us and remain peacefully with him. Let us not leave him alone, let us keep
him company in the best way we can. If we persevere in this exercise, then we shall not delay in dis-
covering the reality of what the Eastern Christians
call "the place of the heart" or the "inner cell."

This interior space of communion with God
exists. It has been granted to us, but many men and
women do not arrive at or even suspect its existence
because they have never entered into this garden to
gather its fruits. Happy are those who have discovered the Kingdom of God within them, for their life
will change.

The human heart is certainly an abyss of misery
and sin, but God lies in its depths. To use an image

---

11. Ibid.

of St. Teresa of Avila: the person who perseveres in prayer is like someone who goes to draw water from a well, throws in the bucket and, at the beginning, gets nothing but mud. However, if he is confident and perseveres, then, one day, he will draw the purest water from his very heart. As the Scripture says, "Out of the believer's heart shall flow rivers of living water" (Jn 7:38).

This is of great importance in our life. If, thanks to perseverance, we discover that "place of the heart," then our thoughts, decisions, and actions, which all too often come from our superficial selves—our discontent, anxiety, and immediate reaction—will gradually proceed from the deepest core of our being where we are united with God in love. We will then acquire a new way of being where everything done is born of love, and thus we shall be truly free.

We have defined four great principles that should guide our behavior during prayer: the primacy of God's action, the primacy of love, the humanity of Jesus as the instrument of communion with God, and God's indwelling in the heart. These serve as points of reference for us to live well our times of prayer.

However, to better understand prayer, we must bear in mind its evolution and the stages of spiritual life.

Chapter Three

The Evolution of the Life of Prayer

The prayer life is not a static but dynamic and evolving reality. It passes through stages and its progress is not always linear. And of course, there are occasional moments of regression!

Spiritual authors usually speak of the development or "stages of prayer," from the habitual to the most elevated, which mark the soul's path toward union with God. St. Teresa of Avila spoke of the seven castles; another author identifies three stages: the purgative, the illuminative, and the unitive. Others point to meditation, followed by affective prayer, the prayer of simply "looking at God and God looking at you," and the prayer of quiet, which precedes the suspension of the faculties in rapture and ecstasy.

We will not attempt a detailed study of the stages of prayer and the graces of the mystical order—or of the trials encountered—though this is much more frequent than generally believed. We leave this to the experts and it is not necessary to address these topics here. Let us add that the various outlines that describe the journey of prayer must not be taken too strictly—as if these were an obligatory path—when the wisdom of God seems to take some pleasure in overturning traditional theories governing the spiritual life.

It is necessary to discuss that which, in our opinion, constitutes the first great stage fundamental to transformation of the life of prayer and from which all subsequent stages proceed.

These stages have different names depending on the criteria and spiritual tradition, and yet we find them everywhere, even if the recommended paths begin at different points. In the West, for example, meditation is generally seen—or used to be seen—as the starting point for prayer. Western tradition speaks about the movement from meditation to contemplation. St. John of the Cross wrote extensively about this phase and the criteria for discerning it.

In the Eastern tradition there is the "Jesus Prayer," also called the "prayer of the heart," popularized in recent years by the book, *Récits d'un pélerin russe (The*

Way of the Pilgrim). This prayer has as its starting point the continuous repetition of a short formula containing the name of Jesus, and leads to the moment when prayer *descends from the mind to the heart.*

In both instances, we are speaking essentially of the same phenomenon, raising the question of whether such transformation [from mind to heart]—described as a simplification of prayer or a passage from "active" to "passive" prayer—can have diverse manifestations, depending on the person and his or her spiritual itinerary.

Of what does this transformation consist? It is a particular gift of God, which is given to the person who has persevered in prayer. We can in no way force this gift; it is a sheer grace, though fidelity to prayer is very important to preparing for and facilitating this grace. This gift may come quickly, sometimes in a few years, or perhaps not at all. At first, the Lord gives it in an almost unseen way. What is more, it may not be a permanent gift, at least at the beginning, and one may advance or regress in it.

The essential characteristic of this gift is that it transforms prayer once dominated by human actions—the voluntary repetition of a formula, as in the case of the Jesus Prayer, or the discursive activity of the mind, as in the case of meditation where affections and resolutions arise from the text or theme reflected upon—into prayer dominated by divine action. In this kind of prayer, the soul does nothing; it allows itself to be acted upon rather than to act by maintaining an attitude of simplicity, abandonment, and loving, serene attentiveness to God.

Such is the case of the Jesus Prayer. One experiences prayer as flowing spontaneously from the heart and placing it in a state of peace, joy, and love. In the case of meditation, this new stage frequently begins with a kind of spiritual aridity, the inability to reflect, and the inclination to remain inactive before God. Nevertheless, this "doing nothing" is not inertia or spiritual laziness, but a loving attitude of abandonment.

This transformation is a great grace even for those long accustomed to saying many things to the Lord or finding joy in meditation. Such persons may feel disillusioned because it seems they are regressing, becoming impoverished in if not incapable of prayer. They are no longer able to pray as they used to, that is, with the help of the intellect and basing their interior discourse on thoughts, images, and feelings.

In his works, St. John of the Cross insists (even criticizes spiritual directors who do not understand this[12]) on convincing those who receive this grace that this poverty is in fact true wealth, and that they must not try to return to meditation. Instead, they ought to content themselves to remain before God in an attitude of self-forgetfulness and with simple, loving, and serene attention.

Why is this poverty true wealth?

Why is this leap to a new stage of prayer such an immense grace? For the simple and basic reason that St. John of the Cross explains so well: all that we understand about God *is not* God; everything we can think, imagine, or feel about God is not God! God is infinitely beyond all of this, thus he transcends any image, representation, or sense perception. Nevertheless, we might say that he is not beyond faith or love. Faith, says the Mystical Doctor, is the only way to prepare ourselves for union with God. That is to say, faith is the only act that brings us to possess God. Faith is a simple and loving movement toward union with God, who reveals himself to us and gives himself to us in Jesus.

In order to approach God in prayer, it is good to make use of mental reflections as well as imagina-

---

12. See in particular, St. John of the Cross, *Living Flame of Love,* stanza E, verse 3.

tion and aspirations for as long as they help us, stimulate and convert us, and strengthen our faith and love. Still, we cannot arrive at the essence of God solely by these means, because God is beyond our intelligence and feelings. Only faith animated by love allows us to reach God. However, we cannot exercise this faith unless there is a kind of detachment from images and sense perceptions. That is why, at a certain point, God withdraws from our senses and it seems that our other faculties no longer function. Faith alone remains.

Thus, the soul is in a situation where it can no longer think or resort to images or feelings, but simply maintains an attitude of loving adherence to God. Even if the soul does not notice any change and perceives it is doing nothing and that nothing is happening, God is already communicating himself secretly, in a deeper and more substantial way.

Prayer is no longer an activity whereby we speak and use our minds and powers to establish contact with God. Now prayer becomes a kind of profound, sometimes felt infusion of love wherein we engage in a mutual dialogue with God. This is the contemplation of which St. John of the Cross speaks: that secret, peaceful, and loving infusion where God gives himself to us. God flows into the soul and the soul flows into God in an almost imperceptible movement as the result of the Holy Spirit's action on the soul.

This phenomenon is difficult to describe in words, but many have experienced it in prayer, sometimes unawares. Jourdain wrote that many simple souls are contemplatives without being conscious of the depth of their prayer. Undoubtedly, it is better this way.

Regardless of the starting point of one's prayer life—and, as we have seen, this can be so diverse— the Lord wants to lead souls to this end or, at least, to this stage. Then the Holy Spirit can lead these souls toward more advanced, elevated stages, which we shall not discuss in this book.

It is striking to note, for example, that in traditions as diverse as the Jesus Prayer and meditation, of which St. John of the Cross is representative, both lead to the same grace of contemplation and use almost analogous expressions. When, for example, St. John of the Cross describes contemplation as a "sweet breath of love,"[13] one recognizes similar language used in the *Philocalia*.[14]

---

13. Ibid.

14. A major work of the Eastern Church, especially in Russia, which compiles the writings of the Fathers of the Church and other spiritual authors.

The Wounded Heart

Now we will consider several points that sum up the preceding chapters and will enable us to appreciate and make concrete the connections between the primacy of love, contemplation, the prayer of the heart, and the humanity of Jesus.

In the final analysis, experience shows that to pray well, to reach a state of passive prayer where God and the soul communicate with each other deeply, *it is necessary for the heart to be wounded* by the love of God, wounded by a thirst for the Beloved. We can descend into the prayer of the heart and dwell there only through this wound of love. God must touch us at the deepest level of our being so that we can no longer proceed without him. Without this wound of love, prayer will never be more than an intellectual activity, that is, a pious spiritual exercise rather than an intimate communion with God, whose heart has been wounded for love of us.

The core of Jesus' humanity as mediator between God and man is his wounded heart. The heart of Jesus was opened so that divine love could pour itself out on us and we could have access to God. But we cannot receive this outpouring of God's love unless our own hearts are opened by a wound. Then a true exchange of love can occur, which is the only goal of prayer. Prayer then becomes what it should be: a heart within a Heart!

The wound of love has different manifestations depending on the situation of the soul. It may be a wound of desire, an anxious search for the Beloved, or one of repentance and sorrow for sin; the wound may be a thirst for God, agony over his absence, a sweetness that expands the heart, an ineffable joy, or an ardent passion. This wound makes us beings marked by God forever, beings who can have no other life than that of God.

Of course, when God reveals himself to us, he seeks to heal us of our bitterness, faults, real or imagined failures, hardness of heart, etc. We know this and we all hope for God's healing, but it is important to understand that, in a certain sense, God seeks to wound us more than to heal us. It is by wounding us more profoundly that he brings us true healing. Whatever God's attitude toward us appears to be, whether he seems to draw near or to be far away, whether he appears tender or indifferent (expect these situations to come up in prayer!), God's objective is always to wound us more with his love.

In his *Treatise on the Love of God,* St. Francis de Sales beautifully illustrates the different means used by God to wound the soul with love. For example, even

when God seems to abandon us to our defects and
spiritual aridity, he does so only to wound us more
deeply with love:

> Take the case of a soul who feels really resolved to
> die rather than to offend God, yet fails to catch the
> slightest spark of fervor; a soul so lacking in the
> feeling of love that it is quite numb, so faint-heart-
> ed that its every step is a fall into evident imperfec-
> tion. That soul, I tell you, is badly wounded; its love
> is deeply pained at God's pretense of being unaware
> that it loves him, at God's seeming abandonment of
> it as though it did not belong to him. Under all its
> defects, its distractions, its coldness, it feels that the
> Lord is leveling this reproach against it: "How can
> you say you love me, when your soul is not in my
> care?" This pain shoots like an arrow through the
> heart; but this pain proceeds from love. If the soul
> were not in love with God, it would not be dis-
> tressed by fear of not loving him.[15]

Sometimes, God wounds us more efficaciously by
leaving us in our poverty than by healing our misery!

Indeed, God seeks less to make us perfect than to
unite us to himself. Perfection, or our own idea
or definition of perfection, would make us self-

---

15. St. Francis de Sales, *The Love of God,* translated and revised
by Vincent Kerns, MSFS (Westminster, Great Britain: Newman
Press, 1962), book 6, chap. 14, pp. 258~259.

sufficient. Instead, to be wounded makes us poor, yet it places us in communion with God. This is what counts: not to acquire an ideal state of perfection but to be unable to live without God, to be so tightly bound to God, in our misery as well as our virtues, that God may unceasingly pour out his love on us and that we may feel the need to give ourselves completely to him because there is no other way! This bond makes us holy and leads us to perfection. This truth explains many things about our spiritual life. It helps us to understand why Jesus did not free St. Paul from his thorn in the flesh, rather, God said to him, "My grace is sufficient for you, for power is made perfect in weakness" (2 Cor 12:9).

This truth also explains why the poor and the lowly, those whom life has wounded, often receive graces in prayer that the powerful do not.

Prayer keeps the wound of love open

Above all prayer consists in keeping the wound of love open. This, too, guides us in knowing what we should do in prayer. When the wound of love runs the risk of closing or shrinking because of routine, lethargy, or the loss of our first fervor, then we ought to react, to awaken our hearts and move them to love by exerting all our effort and employing all the good thoughts and resolutions we can muster. As St. Teresa of Avila would say, we must draw the water we lack until the Lord takes pity on us and sends us some rain.[16] At times, this demands perseverance. "I will rise now and go about the city, in the streets and in the squares; I will seek him whom my soul loves" (Song 3:2). We should surrender to that infusion of love, fulfilling what it requires as a response from us.

As we have already said, there are different starting points for the prayer life, mentioning as examples the practice of meditation and the Jesus Prayer. We live in a time when many people suffer moral and spiritual harm, where God is rejected, and the traditional stages of the spiritual life are upside-down. We often stumble upon the prayer life in an unexpected way and, almost immediately, we receive that wound of love through the grace of conversion, participation in charismatic renewal, some trial sent by Divine Providence, etc. Our role in the life of prayer is to be faithful to it, persevering in that intimate dialogue with God who has touched us with the aim of keeping that wound of love open. We must prevent it from closing when the intense experience of God fades, when God seems far off, and we forget everything that has hap-

---

16. St. Teresa of Avila develops this image extensively in her autobiography, chap. 11ff.

pened, allowing the wound of love to be covered by the dust of routine, doubt, and neglect.

THE HUMAN HEART
AND THE HEART OF THE CHURCH

To conclude this section, we would like to add a few words about the impact of our prayer life on the life of the whole Church. In the first place, dwelling on this beautiful mystery strongly encourages people to persevere in prayer. It also renders void the false impression that our prayer life has little or nothing to do with the life of the Church. On the contrary, there exists an often unseen but extremely profound link between the Church's universal mission and the relationship between God and a soul in the intimacy of prayer. This explains why the Church would proclaim a little Carmelite nun, who never left her convent, patron of the missions.

Much could be said on the subject of the relationship between the Church's mission and how contemplation intimately integrates us into the mystery of the Church and the Communion of Saints.

The grace of prayer always inserts us deeply into the mystery of the Church. This is clear in the Carmelite tradition, which is, in a sense, the most contemplative in a more explicit and radical way, where union with God is sought through a journey of prayer. To the outsider, this spiritual journey may seem individualistic. At the same time, it clearly expresses the connection between the contemplative life and the mystery of the Church. However, this connection is not to be understood in a superficial way, that is, to be judged on visible evidence and immediate results. Rather, it must be grasped in all its mystical depth. The connection is extremely simple but profound: it is born of love, because between God and the soul one can only speak of love, and in the ecclesiology implicit in the doctrine of Carmel's great representatives—Teresa of Avila, John of the Cross, Thérèse of Lisieux—love constitutes the essence of the mystery of the Church. The love that unites God and the soul and the love that constitutes the profound reality of the Church are the same because this love is the gift of the Holy Spirit.

As she was dying, St. Teresa of Avila said, "I am a daughter of the Church." If she established and formed her Carmelites, cloistered her nuns, and led them along the mystical path, she did so in response to the needs of the Church of her time. She was urged on by the ravages wreaked by the Protestant reformation and by the accounts of the conquerors of the great pagan lands in need of being won for Christ. "The world is set afire and this is not about concerning ourselves with trivial things."

For his part, St. John of the Cross very clearly affirms that God's gratuitous and disinterested love experienced in prayer is of greatest benefit to the Church and what she most needs. "An act of pure love benefits the Church more than all the works of the world."

Finally, St. Thérèse of Lisieux describes the most beautiful and perfect bond between personal love for God in prayer and the mystery of the Church. She entered Carmel "to pray for priests and for great sinners." The most critical moment of her life was when she discovered her vocation: she desired all vocations because she wanted to love Jesus to the point of folly and to serve the Church in all possible ways. And her yearning for martyrdom was appeased only when she understood through Sacred Scriptures that the greatest service she could render the Church, and which embraces others, is to keep the fire of love alive.

> ...[W]ithout this love, the missionaries will cease to preach the Gospel, the martyrs will cease to give their life.... At last, I have discovered my vocation: in the heart of the Church, my mother, I will be love!

This is lived above all through prayer:

> I perceive that the more the fire of love sears my heart, the more I will say: Attract me, the more souls approach me (I would be a useless bit of iron if I were to set myself apart from the Divine Fire),

the quicker will they come to the scent of the fragrance of their Beloved, because a soul seared with Love cannot remain inactive. Like Mary Magdalene, who puts herself at the feet of Jesus and hears his sweet and vivid words, though she does not seem to give anything, she gives more than Martha, who worries about many things and wishes her sister to act like her.... All the saints have understood it thus and perhaps especially those who filled the universe with the light of the Gospel. Was it not from prayer that Saints Paul, Augustine, John of the Cross, Thomas Aquinas, Francis, Dominic and many other illustrious friends of God obtained this divine knowledge that fascinated the great geniuses? A wise man said: "Give me a lever and I will move the world." What Archimedes could not do, because he did not direct his request to God and made it from a material point of view, the saints were able to accomplish fully. The Almighty gave them a focal point: HIMSELF and HIMSELF Alone; and as a lever, prayer, which ignites with its fire of love. And that is how the saints moved the world. That is how the saints, still struggling here on earth, move the world, and how future saints will also move the world until the end.[17]

St. Thérèse's life reflects this wondrous mystery: she lived only for a heart-to-heart dialogue with Jesus.

17. See the chapters dedicated to St. Thérèse of Lisieux in the beautiful book by Fr. Léthel, *Connaître l'amour du Christ qui surpasse toute connaissance*, Éditions du Carmel.

The more she entered her heart, the more she centered that heart on Jesus; the more her heart grew, the more she grew in love for the Church. Thérèse's heart grew, like the Church, beyond the limits of space and time. The more Thérèse lived her vocation of spousal love for Jesus through prayer, the more she entered the mystery of the Church. This is the only way to truly understand the Church. One who does not live a spousal relationship with God in prayer will never really understand the Church or grasp her most profound identity as the Spouse of Christ.

In prayer, God communicates with the soul and transmits his desire for all people to be saved. Our hearts are identified with the Heart of Jesus and we share his love for his Spouse, the Church, and his thirst to give his life for the Church and for all people. St. Paul tells us to foster the same sentiments as Christ. However, without prayer it is impossible to achieve identification with Christ.

It is a particular grace of the Carmelite Order to evidence the connection between a profound heart-to-heart relationship with Jesus in prayer and participation in the heart of the Church. No doubt, there is also a Marian grace here. Is not Carmel the first Marian Order of the West? Who other than Mary, the spouse *par excellence* and symbol of the Church, could introduce us to these depths?

Chapter Four

Material Conditions for Prayer

We shall now offer some observations regarding the external conditions for prayer: duration, moments, attitudes, and place.

We should not give undue importance to material conditions or we can fall into the error of being too focused on the unessential or making prayer a matter of technique. In principle, we should pray with the holy freedom of the children of God. It does not matter where, when, or in what physical posture we pray, however we are not pure spirits but creatures of flesh and bone conditioned by our bodies, space, and time. Moreover, on those occasions when the spirit cannot pray, the body, "brother donkey," can fortunately come to the rescue by making a Sign of the

Cross, lying prostrate on the ground, or by the movement of the hands over rosary beads.

TIME

When to pray

Any moment is good for prayer. However, among many possibilities, we should try to give the best time to prayer, when we are relatively alert, not weighed down by pressing concerns, and free of disturbance and repeated interruptions. Still, we often have little freedom to choose the ideal time. Often we are obliged to make the best of the scarce moments between our many commitments. Thus, as much as possible, we must know how to draw benefit from the grace of certain moments favorable for prayer, for example, those after Mass.

This is an important point. We must try to make prayer a habit, part of our regular schedule, and not simply an exceptional moment "stolen" from many other activities. This will make easier fidelity to prayer, which is so fundamental. Human life is a world of rhythm: consider the heartbeat, breathing, meals, the passage from day to night and night to day, the cycle of weeks, months, and years. Prayer must enter into our rhythm so that it may become a habit as vital to our existence as breathing or eating—a "breathing" of the soul. However, we should not understand habit in a negative sense because it is the facility for making natural something that once demanded effort and struggle. Remember, too, that God's place in our life's rhythms and habits is the one he occupies in our heart. And since the basic unit of life's rhythm is a day, prayer should, as much as possible, be done daily.

How long to pray

We ought to dedicate an adequate amount of time to prayer. We are not making time for God if we spend only five minutes in prayer—an amount of time we spend on anything we do not really want to do. The minimum amount of time for prayer is fifteen minutes, but those who have the possibility of spending more time should not hesitate to extend this to an hour a day.

However, we should restrain ourselves from being overly ambitious regarding the duration of prayer and avoid undertaking more than our strength permits. This can only lead to discouragement. It would be better to spend a relatively brief time (twenty to thirty minutes) every day than two hours with less regularity.

Apart from setting a minimum time for prayer, it is also important not to shorten the time except for rare occasions. We would be mistaken to determine the time we spend in prayer according to the pleasure it gives us—if we become bored we set prayer aside. Nevertheless, it would be advisable to take a break from prayer when we become too tired or anxious. In general, however, if we want prayer to yield its fruits, then we must conscientiously stick to that minimum period and not give in to the temptation of cutting it short. Besides, experience shows that the Lord often comes to bless us during the last few minutes of prayer, just as St. Peter experienced in the miraculous catch of fish after spending the whole night without "catching anything."

PLACE

God is present everywhere and, therefore, we can pray anywhere: in a room, in an oratory, before the Blessed Sacrament, in a train, and even while waiting in line at the supermarket.

As much as possible, it is advisable to pray in a place that is conducive to silence and recollection and to attentiveness to God's presence. A chapel with our Lord in the Blessed Sacrament, especially if exposed, is preferable. In this way, we benefit from the grace of the Real Presence.

If we are praying at home, we should try to find an appropriate and tranquil spot with a crucifix or an image of the Blessed Virgin Mary. We need the help of tangible signs—the Word became flesh for this reason. We would do badly to be contemptuous of such images and not surround ourselves with objects that help intensify our devotion. When prayer becomes difficult, a glance at a holy image brings us back to God's presence.

Just as there is a time dedicated to prayer, there should be a place for it in every home. Many families feel the need to have a prayer room or corner in their homes, and it is a good idea.

POSTURE

What is the best posture for prayer? In itself this is not very important because, as we have said, prayer is not a kind of yoga. Our posture while praying depends on our state of health, tiredness, or preference. We can pray sitting, kneeling, prostrate on the ground, standing up, or lying down. Apart from this basic freedom, however, the following suggestions can help.

On the one hand, our physical stance at prayer should permit us a stability or stillness that leads to recollection and allows us to breathe freely. Bad posture causes us to shift and fidget too often, which obviously does not favor the basic disposition of being fully attentive to God's presence.

The body cannot be too relaxed either. If to pray is to pay attention to God's presence, then the body's posture should allow this to happen. The body should not be tense, but the heart must always be oriented toward God. Sometimes, when we are tempted toward laziness or comfort, the posture that best expresses the search and desire for God is kneeling with hands outstretched in supplication. This allows us to find more easily that "attention to God." Once again, we subtly place our "brother donkey" at the service of the spirit.

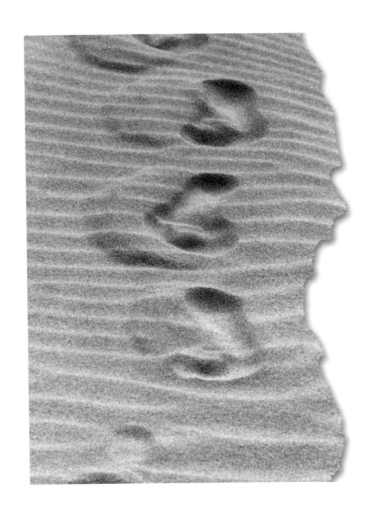

CHAPTER 5

SOME METHODS OF PRAYER

In the light of what has been said, we will now briefly discuss the principal methods of prayer.

There are times, however, when no method is necessary. Nevertheless, it is useful to rely on one or another of the following.

First, we can ask ourselves, "What is the reason for choosing one method over another?" I believe each person is free to choose the most suitable method which he or she adapts to more easily and allows him or her to grow in love for God. Whatever the method, we must make sure to maintain a certain "spiritual climate," which we shall try to describe later. The Holy Spirit will guide us and do all the rest. We must persevere, regardless of the method chosen. There will be dry moments, but we must not hastily drop one method if the desired fruits do not

come right away. At the same time, we must be ready
to disengage ourselves from our customary method,
which may have been good and fruitful for a time,
once the Holy Spirit urges us to set it aside and turn
to another. We cannot be slaves to habit.

Finally, we may combine various methods—for
example, meditation for a part of our prayer and the
Jesus Prayer for another. Still, we have to avoid
capriciously flitting from one method to another.
Prayer ought to incline us to keep still so that an
authentic exchange of love may take place. In prayer,
the movements of love are slow: they commit the
entire being to welcoming God and to self-giving.

MEDITATION

After the sixteenth century, meditation became the
basis for nearly all prayer methods used in the
Western Church.[18] Meditation is a practice that
traces its roots to reading and praying passages from
Sacred Scripture—an ageless custom of the Church
and of the Jewish faith that preceded it. A typical
example is the monastic practice of *lectio divina*.

---

18. It is important to remember this when reading classic authors
such as Teresa of Avila or John of the Cross. We may run the risk of
misunderstanding their teachings as they presume that the reader has
already begun to walk the path of meditation, which can confound
the person who enters prayer through another path.

Meditation consists of a time of structured preparation. We place ourselves in God's presence and invoke the light of the Holy Spirit before choosing a Scripture passage or text from a spiritual writer. We then read the passage slowly, pondering what God is saying to us through the words and how they apply to our life. These considerations ought to enlighten the mind and nourish love in a way that gives rise to affection and resolution.

Here the aim is not to increase our intellectual knowledge but to strengthen our love for God; therefore, we must not rush through *lectio*. We pause on a particular point and "ruminate" on it as long as it nourishes our soul, turning it into a prayer or dialogue with God that is filled with gratitude or adoration. After having exhausted one point, we move on to the next or continue reading. It is advisable to end with a review of all our considerations, thanking God, and asking him to help us put them into action. Numerous books provide themes and methods for meditation. For advice in this regard, it would be good to read the beautiful letter of Fr. Francis Libermann, founder of the Congregation of the Holy Spirit, to his nephew[19] or the counsels of St. Francis de Sales in his *Introduction to the Devout Life*.

---

19. See Appendix I of this book.

Meditation has the advantage of being an accessible method that is easy to start with. It helps us to avoid spiritual laziness because it invites the will to act and allows us to reflect at a personal level.

Meditation also has its risks because it can become more of an exercise of the mind than of the heart. Thus, we can sometimes end up being more attentive to what we are doing than to God himself, or to inadvertently work on our soul simply for the sheer pleasure of it!

Besides, meditation may soon become simply impossible! The soul can no longer read or reflect; but, in general, this is a good sign.[20] This kind of dryness often indicates that the Lord wants to lead the soul to a simpler form of prayer that is more passive yet more profound. As already explained, this is an indispensable step because meditation unites us to God through concepts, images, and feelings.

---

20. St. John of the Cross helps the soul to discern whether this inability to meditate is a sign that God wants to introduce it to a deeper contemplative prayer. This dryness may be due to lukewarmness, whereby the soul loses its taste for the things of God and is more interested in worldly things, or to psychological exhaustion that renders it incapable of being interested in anything at all. One's inability to meditate is God's work if it is accompanied by: (1) a certain inclination to silence and solitude and a desire to be serenely in God's presence; and (2) an aversion to using the imagination for anything that is not God. Cf. *Ascent of Mt. Carmel,* chapter 13.

However, God is beyond all these things and we must be able to set everything aside in order to find God himself, in a simpler but more essential way. The fundamental teaching of St. John of the Cross regarding this form of prayer is not so much to offer counsel on how to make meditation well as to encourage the soul to peacefully abandon it when the moment comes, and to consider this incapacity as a gain and not a loss.

To conclude, we affirm that meditation is good as long as it frees us from our attachment to the world, sin, and lukewarmness, and draws us closer to God. In addition, we must know how to leave it aside when the moment arrives—for divine wisdom, and not us, to decide. Even if meditation is not a habitual practice, it can be helpful in the sense that it helps to shake off laziness or complacency and invites us to actively seek God. Finally, if this method is not or has not been the basis of our prayer, then it still can be a part of our spiritual life in the form of *lectio divina*. For it is indispensable to make a habit of reading Sacred Scripture or spiritual books to nourish our minds and our hearts with the things of God, pausing and praying over the points that strike us.

As a method of prayer, how is meditation viewed today? Certainly, there is no reason to disregard meditation as long as we avoid the obstacles mentioned and use it for our spiritual advancement. However, present-day spiritual experience and sensibility make it a less popular form because many people prefer a simpler, more flexible, and more immediate way of praying.

PRAYER OF THE HEART

In the tradition of the Eastern Church, especially in Russia, the Jesus Prayer, or prayer of the heart, is the way to enter the life of prayer. This pious tradition recently reached the West and has led many souls to interior prayer.

This method consists of repeating a brief formula, which should contain the name of Jesus—the human name of the Incarnate Word—such as, "Lord Jesus, Son of the living God, have mercy on me, a sinner!" This is a manner of praying linked to a beautiful spirituality of the Name, which has biblical roots. A fourth-century saint witnessed to this ancient tradition:

> The most ordinary things were a sign for him to rise to supernatural things. St. Pacomius mentioned a custom of the women of the East: "When I was a child, I saw them chewing betel in order to sweeten their saliva and eliminate

bad breath. The Name of our Lord Jesus Christ should be this for us. If we chew on that blessed name, pronouncing it constantly, [the Lord] imparts in our souls pure sweetness and shows us heavenly things. He is the food of happiness, the source of health, the tenderness of living water, and sweetness of all sweetness. That name which is in the heavens, our Lord Jesus Christ, King of kings, Lord of lords, heavenly reward of all who seek him wholeheartedly, drives away from the soul every evil thought.[21]

The advantage of the Jesus Prayer is that it is simple and very humble. The Eastern Church bears witness to the fact that it can lead one to a life of intense mystical union with God.

We can use the Jesus Prayer anywhere and at any time, even while immersed in our daily concerns, thus allowing us to be in continuous prayer. Over time this prayer becomes a simple invocation of the Name—"Jesus," "Jesus, I love you," or "Jesus, have mercy!"—as the Holy Spirit inspires.

More importantly, as this prayer is a gratuitous gift from God, it cannot be "forced," it descends from "the mind to the heart." Moreover, as it simplifies, we interiorize the prayer in such a way that it becomes

---

21. St. Macarius of Egypt.

almost automatic and enduring, a constant indwelling of the name of Jesus in the heart. Thus, the heart prays ceaselessly and bears his name lovingly. In a way, one lives permanently in the presence of the name of Jesus, from which flow love and peace. "Your name is perfume poured out" (Song 1:3).

The Jesus Prayer is evidently an excellent form of prayer, but it is not meant for everyone. It is certainly a recommended method, since the frequent invocation of the Name takes it into the depths of the heart and mind, uniting the person with God. The Name represents, or rather, makes the Person of Jesus present.

One risk involved in this method is that it can become forced and mechanical, and possibly lead to nervous tension and an agitated repetition of formulas. Therefore, we should practice this method with moderation and gentleness, neither forcing nor prolonging its use. We must allow God to transform it into an interior and flowing prayer, bearing in mind the basic principle that profound prayer is not the fruit of a technique but a grace.

THE HOLY ROSARY

It may surprise some people that the Rosary is presented here as a prayer method. I believe that through it many souls, without realizing it, have reached contemplative and even continuous prayer.

The Rosary is a simple and humble prayer of the poor—and who of us isn't poor? The Rosary is helpful and accessible to everyone, a prayer of intercession that we can pray alone or as a community or within the family. (What could be more natural than to pray a decade of the Rosary for someone's intention?) And, for those who receive the grace, the Rosary can be a prayer of the heart that allows them to enter into union with God in a way similar to the Jesus Prayer. After all, doesn't the Hail Mary contain the name of Jesus?

In the Rosary, Mary invites us to pray. She puts us in touch with the humanity of Jesus and introduces us to the mysteries of her Son. In a certain way, the Rosary allows us to participate in Mary's prayer, which is the most profound.

When prayed slowly and with recollection, the Rosary has the power to put our hearts in communion with God. The heart of Mary leads us to the heart of Jesus. When it is hard to pray and to be recollected in the presence of God, I have often experienced that it suffices for me to pray the Rosary (most of the time without finishing it!) in order to find interior peace and communion with the Lord.

Today, after a period of neglect, the Rosary is coming back with greater force as a precious means of launching into a deep and loving prayer life. This is not a fad or a nostalgic return to an "obsolete" devotion, but a sign of Mary's maternal presence that is felt so strongly in our times. Thanks to this prayer, Mary guides the hearts of all of her children to their Father.

How to Deal with Certain Difficulties

Aridity, monotony, and temptations

Whatever the method, the life of prayer faces many difficulties, among them aridity, lack of enthusiasm, the experience of our miseries, and feelings of futility. These difficulties are inevitable and they should not surprise us or make us anxious. Not only are difficulties inevitable, but they are also beneficial for us because they strengthen our faith and purify our love for God. Therefore, we must welcome them as a grace since through them God sanctifies us and draws us closer to himself. God never permits us to endure a period of trial that does not lead us to abundant grace. As we have said, it is very important not to get discouraged. The Lord, who sees our good will, makes everything work to our benefit.

As for great and persistent difficulties, such as an enduring inability to pray, which may cause us to lose our peace, we should turn to a spiritual director who can reassure and offer us appropriate advice.

Distractions

A most common difficulty is distraction in prayer. It is normal to be distracted, and we should not be surprised or saddened over this. When our mind wanders off, we must not become discouraged or hate ourselves. Rather, we must simply, peacefully, and gently bring our attention back to God. Even if we were to spend an entire prayer period bringing our distracted attention constantly back to God it would not matter. Every time we realize we are distracted in prayer and try to return to the Lord, as poor as it may seem, that prayer is undoubtedly very pleasing to God. God is a Father who knows of what we are made. God does not expect success but good will. It is often more beneficial for us to accept our poverty and powerlessness, without becoming sad or discouraged, than to do everything perfectly.

Besides, except for situations when the Lord acts in this regard, it is impossible to completely control or concentrate the activity of the human spirit, that is, to be completely recollected and free of distraction. Prayer implies recollection; however, it is not a matter of exercising a technique of mental concentration. It would be a mistake to think we could achieve absolute recollection, and we would end up unnecessarily nervous and strained.

Even in the most passive stages of prayer, the spirit remains active. Thoughts arise and the imagination continues to work. The heart may be in a state of tranquil recollection and profound orientation toward God, but the mind continues wandering. Though this can be painful, it does not seriously prevent the heart from uniting itself with God. Such distracting thoughts can come and go like flies, but they do not trouble the recollection of the heart.

When our prayer is still very "cerebral," based primarily on intellectual activity, then distractions can be vexing, because they stop us from praying. However, if, by God's grace, we have entered a more profound prayer of the heart, then distractions cease to become bothersome. The spirit can be somewhat distracted (and, in fact, in general it will always be marked by a coming and going of thoughts), but this will not prevent the heart from praying.

Thus, the real solution to the problem of distractions is not that we concentrate more but that we love more intensely.

I have said so much, and yet so very little.... I simply wish that this book help people to launch out on the path of prayer and to persevere on it. May the reader put these suggestions into practice and let the Holy Spirit take care of the rest.

To those who wish to deepen their understanding of these themes, I suggest that they refer to the writings of the saints, especially those cited herein. It is better to go directly to them and their writings, as these offer profound and enduring counsels. Too many admirable treasures useful to Christians lie dormant in libraries. If we were more familiar with the masters of Christian spirituality, fewer young people would feel the need to go after gurus to slake their thirst for the spiritual.

APPENDIX I

Method for meditation as proposed by Fr. Francis Libermann, Founder of the Congregation of the Holy Spirit [Spiritan Fathers], in a letter to his 15-year-old nephew, Francis, teaching him how to pray.[22]

I bless God for the good desires that he inspires in you and I can only encourage you to apply yourself to mental prayer. Here is, more or less, the method that you may follow to accustom yourself to prayer. First of all, each evening read some pious book that best suits your interests and needs, be it, for example, on the way to practice virtues or about the life and example of our Lord Jesus Christ or the Most Blessed Virgin. At night, go to sleep with these good thoughts and in the morning, when you get up, try to recall the pious reflections which will comprise the subject of your prayers. After your vocal prayer, place yourself in God's presence; think that this great

---

22. *Lettres du venerable Pére Libermann*, L. Vogel (Paris: DDB, 1964).

God is everywhere, that he is where you are, that he is, in a particular way, deep inside your heart, and adore him. Then, remember who you are, that you are unworthy, because of your sins, to appear before his infinitely holy Majesty. Humbly ask him to pardon your sins, make an act of contrition, and recite the *Confiteor*. Finally, acknowledge that you are incapable, by yourself, of praying the way God wants you to. Invoke the Holy Spirit; ask him to come to your aid and teach you to pray well, and pray, *Come, Holy Spirit*. In this way, your prayer will begin. It has three points: adoration, reflection, and resolution.

First: Adoration

You will begin to fulfill your homage to God, our Lord Jesus Christ, or the Most Blessed Virgin, depending on the subject of your meditation; thus, for example, if you meditate on the perfection of God or on a virtue, you render homage to God, who possesses an infinitely higher level of perfection, or our Lord who practiced this virtue so perfectly. If you pray about humility, for example, you will consider how humble our Lord was, he, who was God from all eternity and who lowered himself unto becoming a child born in a manger, obeying Joseph and Mary for many years; unto the washing of his apostles' feet and suffering all kinds of insults and outrage from men.

Thus, you will express your awe of him, your love, and your gratitude. You will stir up your heart to love him and to desire to imitate him. You can also consider this virtue in the Most Blessed Virgin or any saint and see how they practiced it, and show to the Lord your desire to imitate them.

If you meditate on the mystery of our Lord, for example the Nativity, picture yourself in the place where it happened and the persons found there. You will imagine, for instance, the cave where the Savior was born, the Child Jesus in the arms of Mary and with St. Joseph beside them, the shepherds, and the Magi who came to worship him. Then, you will unite yourself to them in adoring and praising him, in prayer.

You can also use similar images when you meditate upon the great truths, like hell, the last judgment, and death. For instance, you might imagine that you are dying. Imagine the people who might surround you—a priest, your parents—and your own feelings at such a time, and you might produce the affections toward God that you would have at that moment: fear and confidence, etc. After dwelling on these affections and sentiments, for as long as you desire and as long as you feel yourself usefully occupied, then you will proceed to the second point, which is that of reflection.

Second: Reflection

Now, you will serenely examine in your soul the principal motives that should convince you of the truth upon which you are meditating. For example, of the necessity to work for your salvation if it is on salvation that you meditate, or the rationale that should compel you to love and practice this virtue. For example, if you are praying about humility, then you could consider the many reasons that compel you to be humble. In the first place is the example of our Lord, the Most Blessed Virgin, and all the saints. Then, because pride is the origin and cause of all sins, while humility is the foundation of all virtues. Finally, because there is nothing in you that should cause you to be vain. What do you have that you have not received from God? Life and its preservation, sanctity of soul, and good thoughts, everything comes from God. You have nothing which should cause you to glorify yourself. On the contrary, you have every reason to humble yourself, thinking of the many times you have offended God, your Savior, your Benefactor.

To make these reflections, do not seek to remember all the reasons that could have convinced you of this or that truth or to practice this or that virtue. Pause only on some that strike you most and would serve you best in practicing a given virtue. Make these reflections gently, without tiring your spirit. When a given reflection ceases to make a strong impression on you, move on to another. Intermingle with these reflections pious affection for our Lord and the desire to please him. From time to time offer him short prayers and aspirations and the good desires of your heart.

After having reflected on the motives, you will enter into the depths of your conscience and carefully examine how you have conducted yourself until that moment as regards the truth or virtue on which you have meditated. For instance, if you have meditated on humility, what are the faults you have committed, the circumstances surrounding that fall, and what means can you employ so as not to fall again. Then you will move on to the third point, which is to formulate some resolutions.

Third: Resolutions

Good resolutions are among the greatest fruits you ought to gather from your prayer. Remember, it is not enough to say: I will not be proud again. I will not praise myself. I will not be ill humored. I will be charitable with everyone, etc.

Without doubt, these are excellent desires that show a good disposition of soul. However, you must take a further step. You must ask yourself under what circumstances during the day you risk falling into the very fault you have decided to avoid, as well as the circumstances you can hope to practice the corresponding virtue. For example, if you have meditated on humility, examine yourself and you may realize that when you are questioned in class, you feel a great self-love and the desire to be admired. Then you will resolve to recollect yourself a moment before being called upon to make an act of interior humility and to tell the Lord that with all your heart you renounce any feeling of self-love that rises up within you. If you have noticed that you engage in frivolous conduct under certain circumstances, then resolve to avoid such occasions, if you can, or recollect yourself a bit at the moment when this might occur. If you realize you have a certain antipathy toward someone, then resolve to talk to that person and show him your friendship. And so on with regard to the rest.

Still, while the many and excellent resolutions you make are good, everything would be useless if God did not come to your help. Ask insistently for God's grace. Do so after making your resolutions, and even while you are making them, in order that God would help you to be faithful to them. Do this at other moments of your prayer. In general, your meditation does not have to be dry and only the work of your mind. Your heart must expand before such a good Master, like the heart of a child before a father who loves him tenderly. To render your petitions more fervent and effective, you should lovingly tell the Lord that you seek the grace to practice the virtue on which you have meditated; that it is for his glory and to fulfill his will as the angels in heaven do; that you need his help to be faithful to these good resolutions; and that you ask this grace in the name of his beloved Son, Jesus Christ, who died on the cross so that you might merit these graces; that he promised to heed all those who ask in the name of his Son.

Place yourself, too, under the protection of the Most Blessed Virgin. Pray that this good Mother intercede for you. She is all-powerful and all good. She does not know how to say "No," and God grants her all that she asks on our behalf. Pray also to your patron saint and your Guardian Angel. Their prayers cannot fail to obtain for you graces, virtues, and fidelity to your resolutions.

During the day, remember to renew your good resolutions in order to put them into practice or to examine whether you have observed them well. Lift your heart to the Lord from time to time so as to renew the good dispositions he placed in your heart during the morning's prayer. Rest assured that by acting in this way you will benefit immensely from this pious exercise and that you will make great progress in virtue and in love for God.

Do not let distractions disturb you. As soon as you perceive a distraction, reject it and peacefully continue to pray. It is impossible not to have distractions. The only thing God asks is that we return faithfully to him every time we notice that we are distracted. These will gradually diminish and your prayer will become sweeter and easier.

My beloved nephew, these are the instructions that I believe are suited to facilitating the necessary practice of prayer. They are the great means all the saints used. I hope that, with the help of grace, you will also benefit from them. May your good will be rewarded with graces from this good Master.

Appendix II

*Letter of Brother Lawrence of the Resurrection
(1614–1691) on living in God's presence.*[23]

The most holy and necessary practice in the spiritual life is to live in the presence of God. This consists in taking pleasure in God's divine company, speaking humbly and remaining lovingly with him at all times, unconcerned about rules or measure, and above all in times of temptation, sorrow, dryness, disillusionment, and even amidst sin and infidelity.

We must apply ourselves to this continually in order to transform our actions into small, uncomplicated conversations with God, flowing from pure and simple hearts.

We must weigh and measure all our actions, without the impetuosity or rashness that mark an indulgent spirit. We must work by God's side with love

---

23. Excerpt from the book, *L'expérience de la présence de Dieu* by Brother Lawrence of the Resurrection (Le Seuil).

and serenity, asking him to be pleased with our efforts. Thanks to this continual attention to God's presence, we shall crush the devil's head and disarm him.

We must, during out work and other actions, even during our reading, however spiritual, during our external devotions and vocal prayers, pause for a moment, as often as we can, to adore God from the depths of our hearts, to taste him in passing, as if to take him by surprise, praise him, ask for his help, offer him our hearts, and thank him.

What could be more pleasing to God than to withdraw from all creatures a thousand times a day just to adore him from within our hearts?

We cannot offer God a greater homage of fidelity than that of renouncing and despising creatures thousands of times in order to rejoice in the Creator for a single instant. This practice slowly destroys our self-love, which cannot subsist except among fellow creatures, and which this frequent turning to God removes from us. (LK 5:15)

We do not always have to be in church to be with God. We can turn our hearts into oratories where we can withdraw and seek friendly conversation with him. We are all capable of these familiar encounters with God. A small elevation of the heart suffices...a small remembrance of God, an interior act of adoration, perhaps even while advancing with sword in hand.[24] Prayer, no matter how brief, is very pleasing to God. Far from causing us to lose courage in perilous situations, prayer strengthens us. Remember this as many times as possible. This is the best way to pray, and a necessary one at that for a soldier who is always in danger of losing his life and, frequently, his salvation.

Living in God's presence is a remarkable help for praying well because, in preventing the mind from straying during the day and keeping it close to the presence of God, it will be easier for the spirit to be calm and quiet during prayer....

24. Brother Lawrence wrote to counsel a young gentleman, a soldier, about this exercise.

BOOKS & MEDIA

The Daughters of St. Paul operate book and media centers at the following addresses. Visit, call or write the one nearest you today, or find us on the World Wide Web, www.pauline.org

CALIFORNIA

3908 Sepulveda Blvd, Culver City, CA 90230	310-397-8676
5945 Balboa Avenue, San Diego, CA 92111	858-565-9181
46 Geary Street, San Francisco, CA 94108	415-781-5180

FLORIDA

145 S.W. 107th Avenue, Miami, FL 33174	305-559-6715

HAWAII

1143 Bishop Street, Honolulu, HI 96813	808-521-2731
Neighbor Islands call:	800-259-8463

ILLINOIS

172 North Michigan Avenue, Chicago, IL 60601	312-346-4228

LOUISIANA

4403 Veterans Memorial Blvd, Metairie, LA 70006	504-887-7631

MASSACHUSETTS

885 Providence Hwy, Dedham, MA 02026	781-326-5385

MISSOURI

9804 Watson Road, St. Louis, MO 63126	314-965-3512

NEW JERSEY

561 U.S. Route 1, Wick Plaza, Edison, NJ 08817	732-572-1200

NEW YORK

150 East 52nd Street, New York, NY 10022	212-754-1110

PENNSYLVANIA

9171-A Roosevelt Blvd, Philadelphia, PA 19114	215-676-9494

SOUTH CAROLINA

243 King Street, Charleston, SC 29401	843-577-0175

TENNESSEE

4811 Poplar Avenue, Memphis, TN 38117	901-761-2987

TEXAS

114 Main Plaza, San Antonio, TX 78205	210-224-8101

VIRGINIA

1025 King Street, Alexandria, VA 22314	703-549-3806

CANADA

3022 Dufferin Street, Toronto, ON M6B 3T5	416-781-9131

¡También somos su fuente para libros, videos y música en español!